UK MU HAI OF FAM

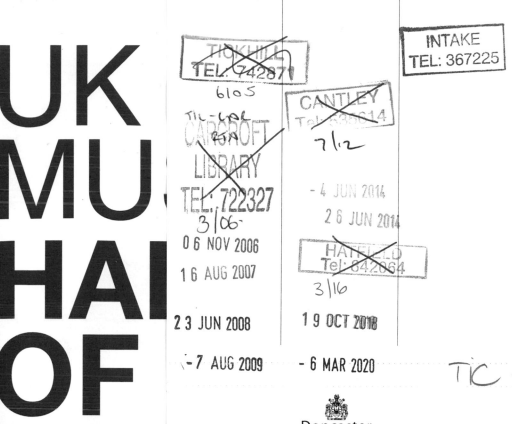

Published by
Wise Publications
8/9 Frith Street, London, W1D 3JB, England.

Exclusive Distributors:
Music Sales Limited
Distribution Centre, Newmarket Road,
Bury St Edmunds, Suffolk, IP33 3YB, England.
Music Sales Pty Limited
120 Rothschild Avenue, Rosebery, NSW 2018, Australia.

Order No. AM91956
ISBN 0-7119-4072-X
This book © Copyright 2005 by Wise Publications.

Unauthorised reproduction of any part of this publication by
any means including photocopying is an infringement of copyright.

Music arranged by Paul Honey.
Music processed by Paul Ewers Music Design.
Music edited by Lucy Holliday.
Printed in the United Kingdom.

www.musicsales.com

Your Guarantee of Quality
As publishers, we strive to produce every book to the highest
commercial standards. Whilst endeavouring to retain the original running
order of the recorded album, the book has been carefully designed to
minimise awkward page turns and to make playing from it a real pleasure.
Particular care has been given to specifying acid-free, neutral-sized
paper made from pulps which have not been elemental chlorine
bleached. This pulp is from farmed sustainable forests and
was produced with special regard for the environment.
Throughout, the printing and binding have been planned to ensure a
sturdy, attractive publication which should give years of enjoyment.
If your copy fails to meet our high standards, please inform us
and we will gladly replace it.

Wise Publications
part of The Music Sales Group
London/New York/Paris/Sydney/Copenhagen/Berlin/Madrid/Tokyo

RADIO GAGA

Words & Music by Roger Taylor

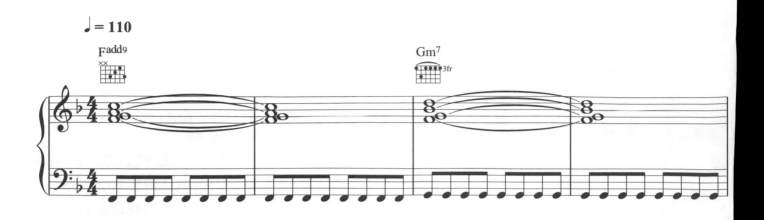

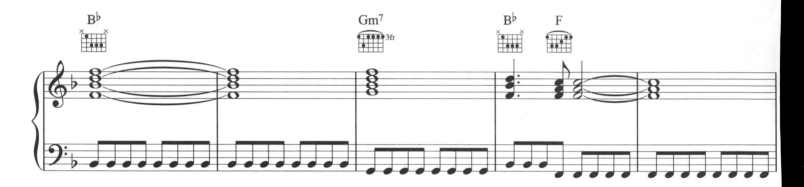

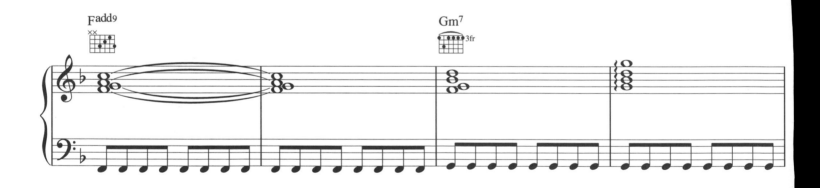

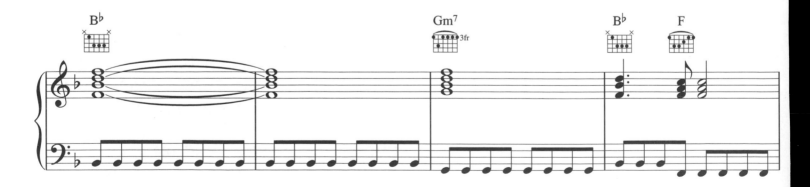

3

(F)

2. We

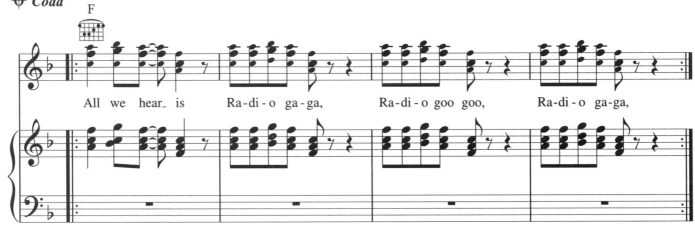

⊕ *Coda*

All we hear_ is Ra-di-o ga-ga, Ra-di-o goo goo, Ra-di-o ga-ga,

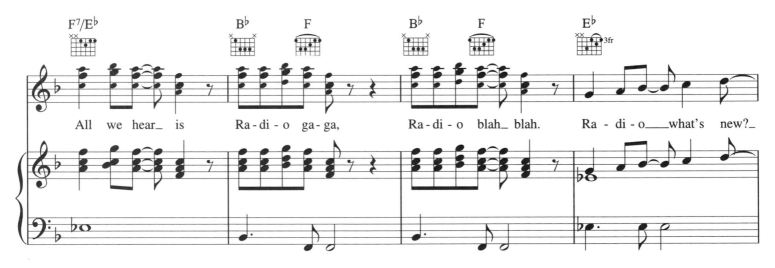

F⁷/E♭   B♭   F   B♭   F   E♭

All we hear_ is Ra-di-o ga-ga, Ra-di-o blah_ blah. Ra-di-o___what's new?_

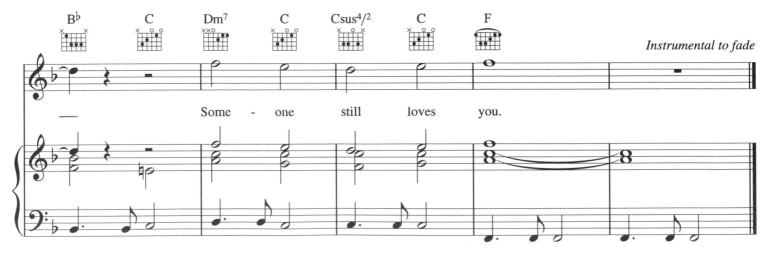

B♭   C   Dm⁷   C   Csus⁴/²   C   F

Instrumental to fade

___ Some - one still loves you.

ELECTRICAL STORM

Words by Bono
Music by U2

1. The sea, it swells___ like a sore___ head,___ and the night it___ is ach-

all of the time,___ I know that's not e - nough.___

If the sky can crack___ there must be some way back___ for love and on-

-ly love. E - lec - tri - cal storm.___ E - lec-

- tri - cal___ storm.___ Ba - by don't

cry.___   2. Car   a - larm,___   won't

let you___ go to sleep.   You're kept a - wake,   dream - ing some - one els - es dream.___

___ Cof - fee is cold,   but it -'ll___ get you___ through.   Com - pro - mise, that's
(3° see block lyrics)

no - thing new to you.___   Let's see   col - ours that have nev - er been   seen.___

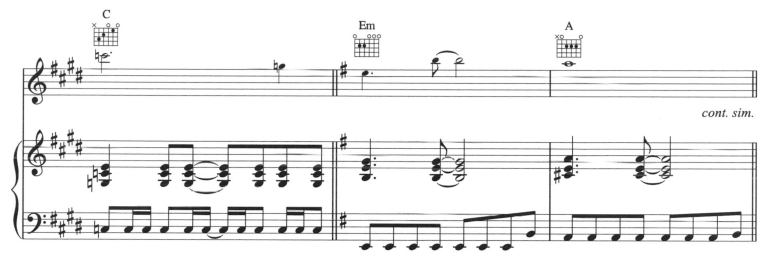

cont. sim.

Ba - by don't_____ cry._____ Ba - by don't_____

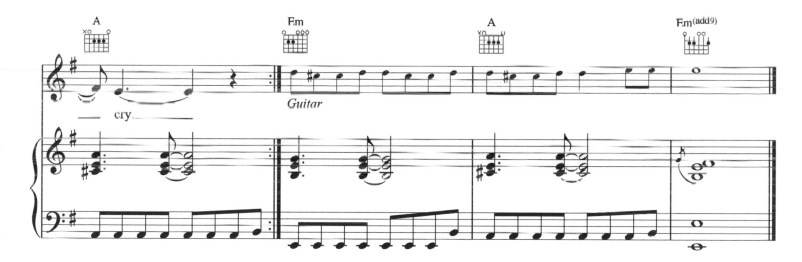

_____ cry._____ *Guitar*

℗:
It's hot as hell honey, in this room
Sure hope the weather will break soon
The air is heavy, heavy as a truck
Need the rain to wash away our bad luck.

Hey, hey.

Well if the sky can crack *etc.*

DANCING IN THE DARK

Words & Music by Bruce Springsteen

1. I get up in the eve - ning,___ and I ain't___ got no - thing to say.
2. Mes - sages keeps get - ting clear - er,___ radio's on and I'm mov - ing___ 'round the place.
3. Stay on the streets of this___ town, and they'll be carv - ing you___ up all right.

I come home in the morn - ing, I go to bed feel -
I check my look in the mir - ror, I wan - na change my clothes,___
They say you got to stay hun - gry, hey ba - by I'm just a - bout

ORANGE CRUSH

Words & Music by Peter Buck, Michael Stipe, Michael Mills & William Berry

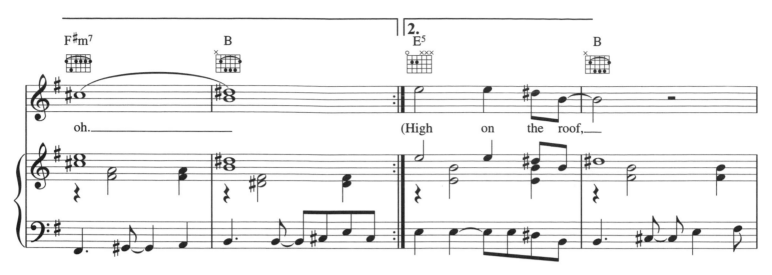

oh._____

(High on the roof,____

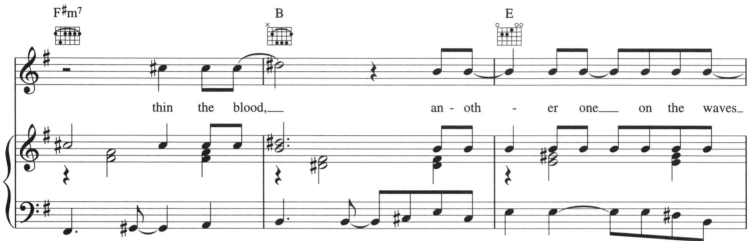

thin the blood,____ an - oth - er one____ on the waves___

_____ to - night,___ com - ing in, you're home.)___

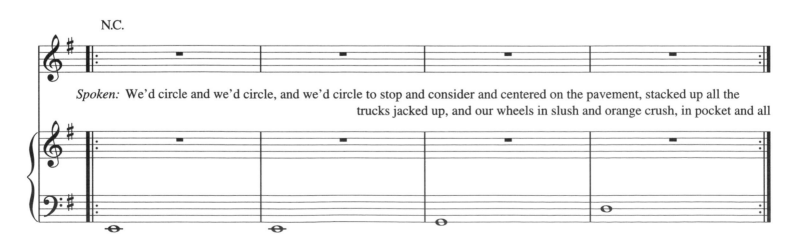

N.C.

Spoken: We'd circle and we'd circle, and we'd circle to stop and consider and centered on the pavement, stacked up all the trucks jacked up, and our wheels in slush and orange crush, in pocket and all

this here country - hell, any country - it's just like heaven here and I was remembering, and I was just in a different country and all then this whirlybird, that I headed for I had my goggles pulled off. I knew it all, I knew every back road and every truck stop.

D.S. al Coda

Coda

High on the roof,

thin the blood, an oth er one on the waves

to - night, com - ing in you're home.

PURPLE HAZE

Words & Music by Jimi Hendrix

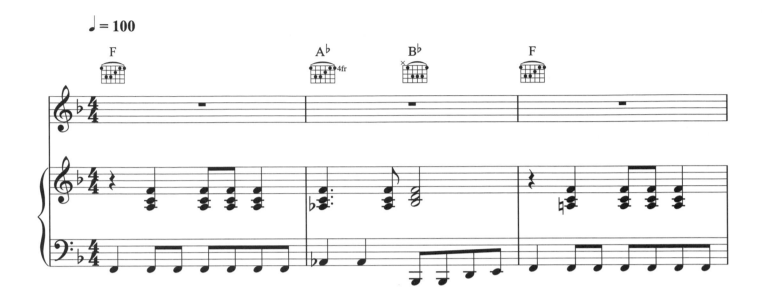

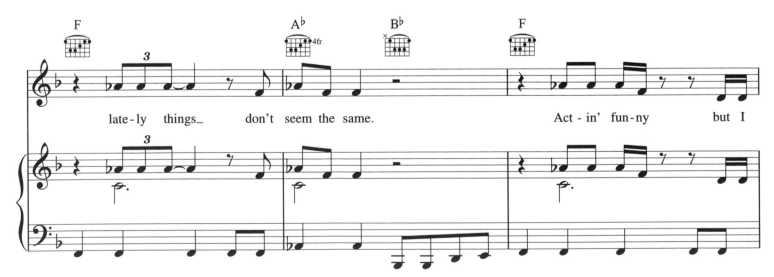

don't know why,   'scuse me___   while I   kiss the sky.

Pur-ple haze___   all a- round,

don't know   if I'm com - in' up or down,   am I hap - py   or

in mi - se - ry?___   What - ev - er it is,___ that girl   put a

LET ME ENTERTAIN YOU

Words & Music by Robbie Williams & Guy Chambers

Lyrics:

1. Hell is gone and Heaven's here, there's nothing left for you to fear, shake your arse come over here, now scream. I'm a burning effigy of ev'rything I used to be you're my rock of empathy my dear. So come on

2. Life's too short for you to die so grab yourself an alibi heaven knows your mother lied, mon cher. Separate your right from wrongs come and sing a different song the kettle's on so don't be long mon cher. So come on

let me_____ en - ter - tain___ you,

let me_____ en - ter - tain___ you.

Look me up in the yel - low pa - ges I will be your rock of a - ges, you

see through fads and your cra - zy pha - ses, yeah.

Lit - tle Bo Peep has lost his sheep, he

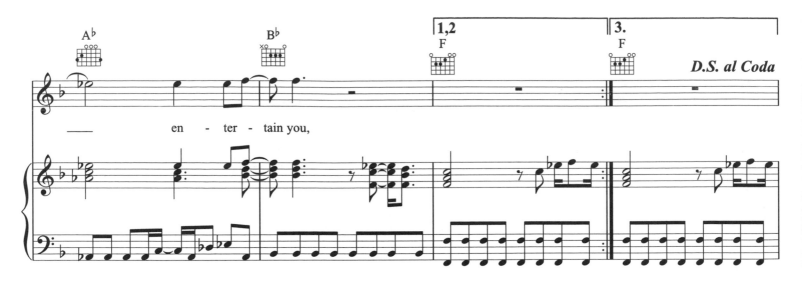

en - ter - tain you,

D.S. al Coda

Coda

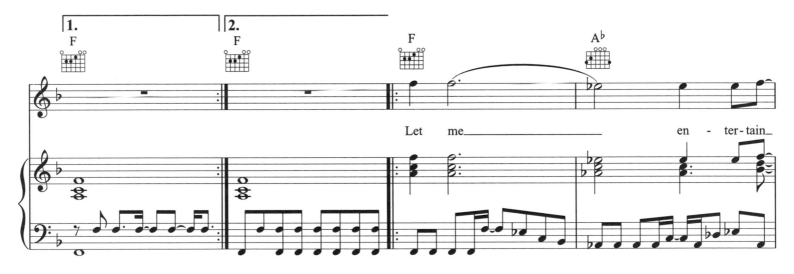

Let me_____ en - ter - tain_

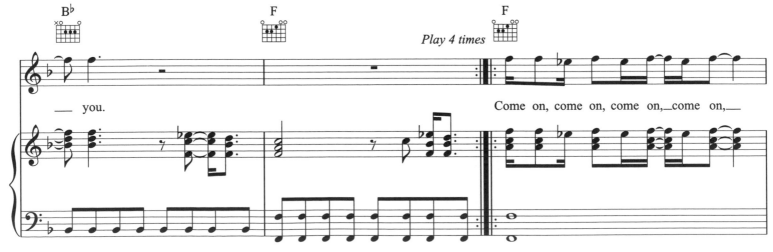

_ you.

Play 4 times

Come on, come on, come on,_come on,_

come on, come on, come on,__ come on,__ come on, come on, come on,__ come on,__

play 3 times and fade

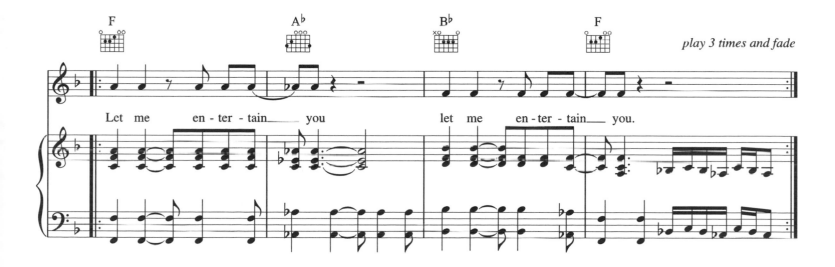

Lct me en-ter-tain__ you let me en-ter-tain__ you.

VOGUE

Words & Music by Madonna Ciccone & Shep Pettibone

Moderate dance beat ♩ = 116

What you look-in' at?__ Vogue, Vogue, Vogue.

Vogue, Vogue, Vogue.

1. Look a-round, ev-'ry-where you turn is heart-ache, it's ev-'ry-where that you go.__
2. All you need is your own i-ma-gi-na-tion, so use it, that's what it's for.__

You try ev-'ry-thing you can to es-cape
Go in-side, for your fi-nest in-spi-ra-tion,

the pain of life that you know.__ When all__ else fails,__ and you
your dreams will op-en the door.__ It makes no diff-'rence if you're

long to be__ some-thing bet-ter than you are to-day.__
black or white,__ if you're a boy or a girl.__ If the

I know a place where you can get a-way,_ it's called a dance floor and here's what_
mu-sic's pump-in', it will give you new life._ You're a su-per-star, yes, that's what_

_ it's for,_ so
_ you are_ you know it. } Come on, Vogue,_ let your bo-dy

move_ to the mu - sic, hey, hey,_ hey.

Come on, Vogue,_ let your bo-dy

to the mu - sic. Ooh,_____

— you've got to just let your bo - dy go_____ with the flow._

Oh,_____ you've got to:

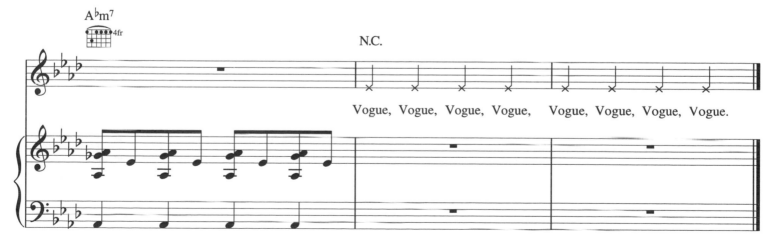

Vogue, Vogue, Vogue, Vogue, Vogue, Vogue, Vogue, Vogue.

FASTLOVE

Words & Music by George Michael

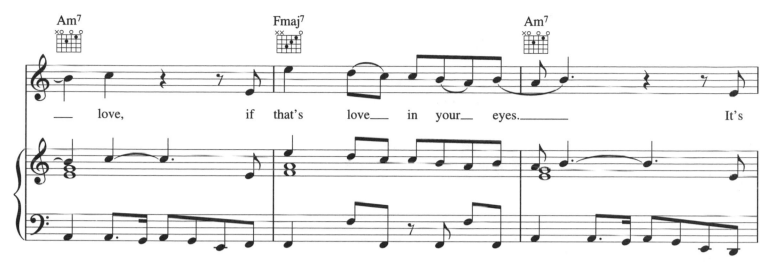

love, if that's love in your eyes. It's

more than in love, had some bad luck, so fast love is all

that I've got on my mind.

Vocals ad lib.

Instrumental ad lib.

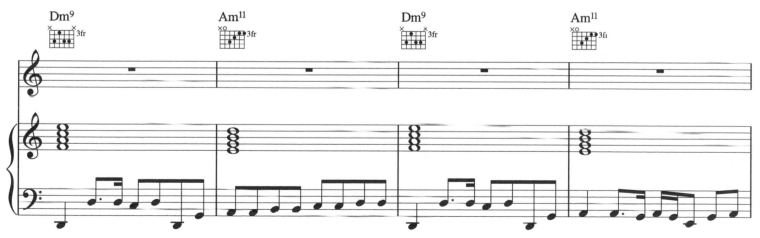

LIVE AND LET DIE

Words & Music by Paul McCartney & Linda McCartney

When you were young and your heart was an op-en book,

*2° Instrumental till ***

you used to say live and let live. (You know you did, you know you did, you know you

did.)__ But if this ev-er-chang-ing world in which we live in makes you give it a try,__

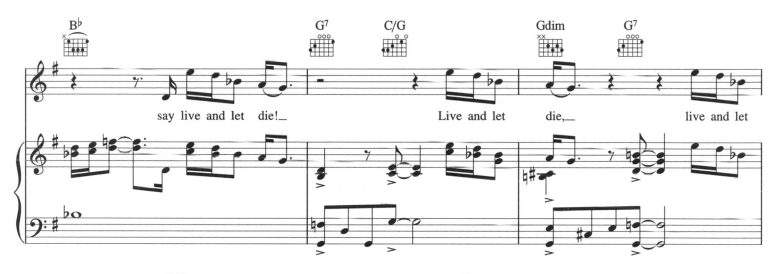

say live and let die!__ Live and let die,__ live and let

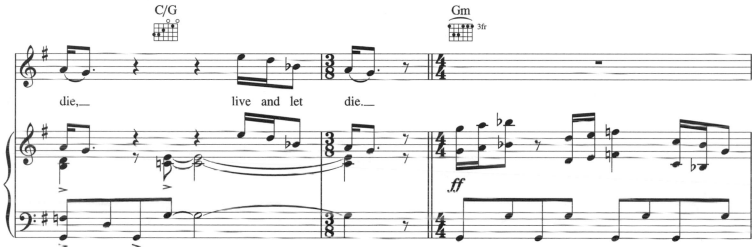

die,__ live and let die.__

To Coda ⊕

What does it mat - ter to ya, when you got a job to do__ you got - ta

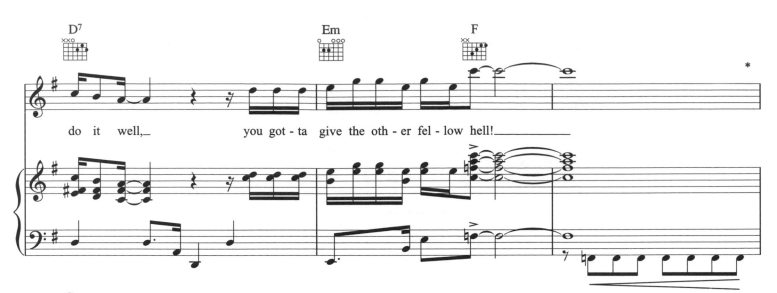

do it well,_____ you got - ta give the oth - er fel - low hell!_____

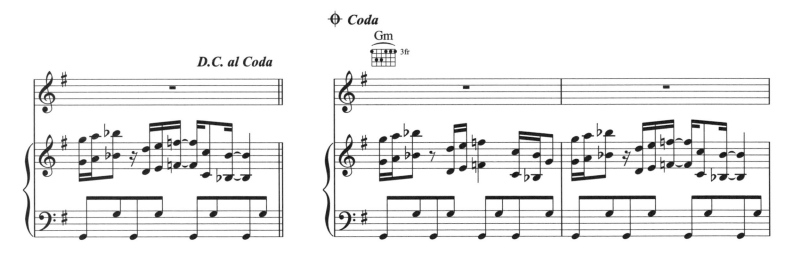

A BOY NAMED SUE

Words & Music by Shel Silverstein

- fore he left, he went and named me Sue.

Well he must have thought it was quite a joke, and it got a lot of laughs from a

lot of folks. It seems I had to fight my whole life through.

Some gal would giggle and I'd get red, and some guy would laugh and I'd

Verse 2:

(Well,) I grew up quick and I grew up mean. My fist got hard and my wits got keen.
Roamed from town to town to hide my shame, but I made me a vow to the moon and stars,
I'd search the honky tonks and bars and kill that man that give me that awful name.
But it was Gatlinburg in mid July and I had just hit the town and my throat was dry,
I thought I'd stop and have myself a brew. At an old saloon on a street of mud
There at a table dealing stud sat the dirty, mangy dog that named me Sue.

Verse 3:

Well I knew that snake was my own sweet dad from a worn out picture that my mother had had.
And I know that scar on his cheek and his evil eye. He was big and bent and grey and old
And I looked at him hard and my blood ran cold, and I said "My name is Sue. How do you do.
Now you're gonna die." Yeah, that's what I told him.
Well I hit him hard right between the eyes and he went down, but to my surprise he came up with a knife
And cut off a piece of my ear. But I busted a chair right across his teeth, and we crashed through
The wall and into the street, kicking and a-gouging in the mud and the blood and the beer.

Verse 4:

I tell you I've fought tougher men but I really can't remember when,
He kicked like a mule and he bit like a crocodile. I heard him laughin' and then him cussin',
He went for his gun and I pulled mine first. He stood there looking at me and I saw him smile,
And he said "Son, this world is rough and if a man's gonna make it, he's gotta be tough
And I know I wouldn't be there to help you along. So I give you that name and I said 'Goodbye,'
I knew you'd have to get tough or die. And it's that name that helped to make you strong."

Verse 5:

Yeah, "He said now you just fought one helluva fight, and I know you hate me and you've
Got the right to kill me now and I wouldn't blame you if you do. But you ought to thank me
Before I die for the gravel in your guts and the spit in your eye because I'm the son of a bitch
That named you Sue."
Yeah, what could I do? What could I do?
I got all choked up and I threw down my gun. Called him my pa and he called me his son,
And I come away with a different point of view. And I think about him now and then.
Every time I tried, every time I win and if I ever have a son I think I'm gonna name him
Bill or George, any damn thing but Sue'.

51

GOODBYE YELLOW BRICK ROAD

Words & Music by Elton John & Bernie Taupin

Moderately (Swung ♪'s)

1. When are you gon-na come down, when are you going to land?___ I
(Verse 2 see block lyric)

should have stayed___ on the farm,___ should have list-ened to my___ old man.___ You

know you can't hold me for- ev - er, I did- n't sign up with you. I'm

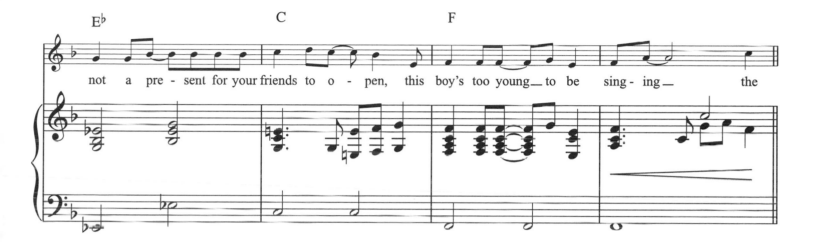

not a pre - sent for your friends to o - pen, this boy's too young to be sing - ing the

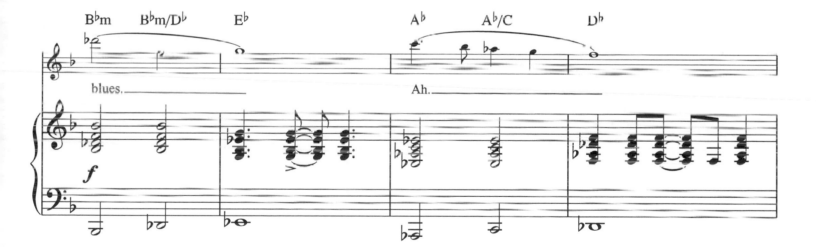

blues. Ah.

Ah. So good- bye yel- low brick road, where the

dogs of so - ci - et - y howl___ You can't plant me in your pent - house,___ I'm

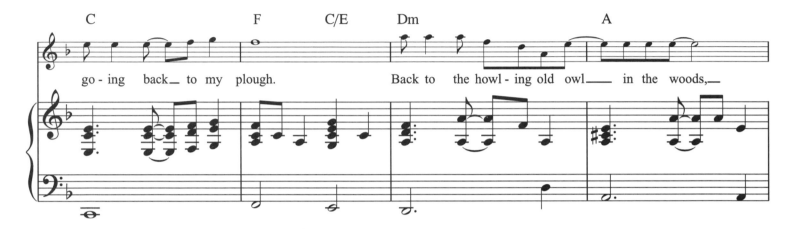

go - ing back___ to my plough. Back to the howl - ing old owl___ in the woods,___

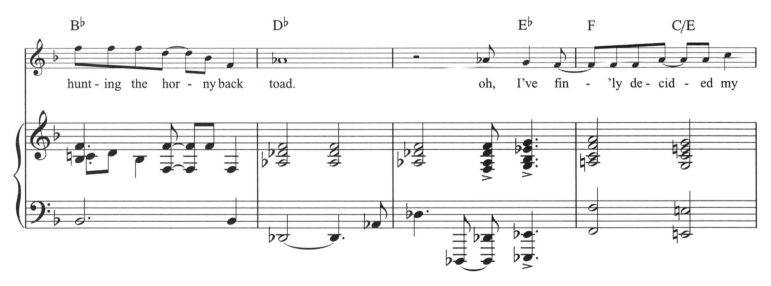

hunt - ing the hor - ny back toad. oh, I've fin - 'ly de - cid - ed my

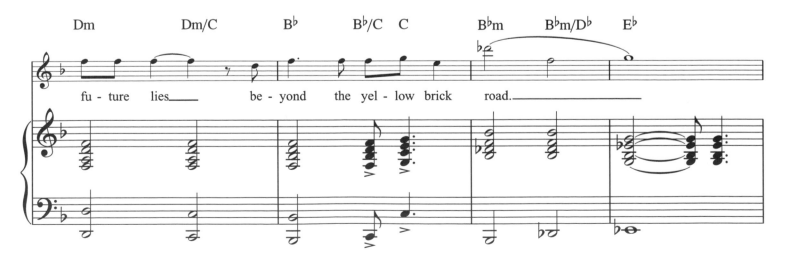

fu - ture lies___ be - yond the yel - low brick road.___

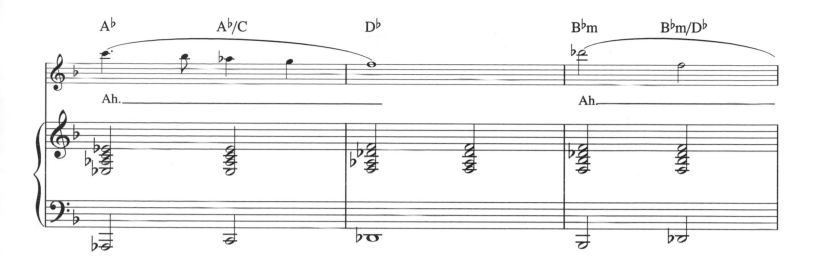

Verse 2:

What do you think you'll do then?
I bet that'll shoot down your plane.
It'll take you a couple of vodka and tonics
To set you on your feet again.
Maybe you'll get a replacement,
There's plenty like me to be found.
Mongrels who ain't got a penny
Singing for titbits like you on the ground.
Ah, ah.

So goodbye yellow brick road, *etc.*

MRS. ROBINSON

Words & Music by Paul Simon

De de de de de de de de de de de de de.___

Do do do do do

do   do   do   do.____

E   A   D   A/C#

De de de de   de   de   de dc   de____   de de de   de.__

Bm   F#

E7

And   here's   to   you_

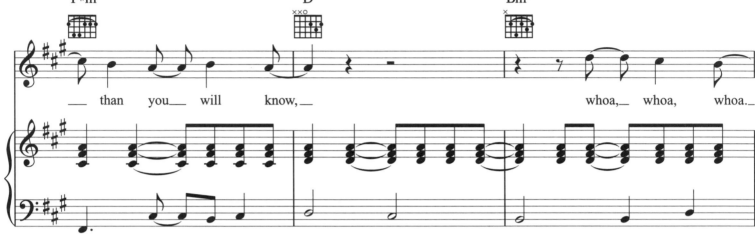

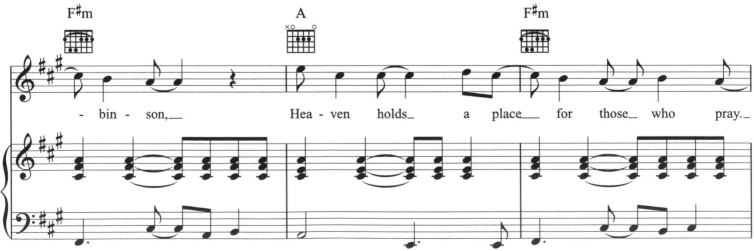

58

Hey,___ hey, hey.___

Hey___ hey hey.___

To Coda ⊕ F#7

1. We'd like to know___ a lit-
(Verses 2 & 3 see block lyric)

-tle bit a - bout___ you for___ our files.___

We'd like to help you learn to help your-
-self.
Look a-round you, all you need are sym-pa-the-tic eyes.
Stroll a-round the grounds un-

- til you feel at home.___ And here's to you___ Where have you gone___

Verse 2:
Hide it in a hiding place
Where no one ever goes
Put it in your pantry
With your cup cakes
It's a little secret
Just the Robinsons affair
Most of all you've got to hide it from the kids.

Koo koo kachoo Mrs. Robinson *etc.*

Verse 3:
Sitting on a sofa
On a Sunday afternoon
Going to the candidates debate
Laugh about it
Shout about it when you've got to choose
Every way you look at this you lose.

Where have you gone Joe Di Maggio
A nation turns it's lonely eyes to you
Ooh ooh ooh
What's that you say Mrs. Robinson
Jolting Joe has left and gone away
Hey hey hey
Hey hey hey.

SUBTERRANEAN HOMESICK BLUES

Words & Music by Bob Dylan

badge out, laid off, says he's got a bad cough; wants to get it paid off.

D7   A7

Look out, kid, __ it's some-thin' you did; __ God knows when __ but you're

do - in' it a - gain! You bet - ter duck down the al - ley - way

E7

look - in' for a new friend; the man in the coon - skin cap by the big pen

63

wants e - lev - en dol - lar bills: You on - ly got ten.

(after last verse, repeat intro and fade)

Verse 2:
Maggie comes fleet foot
Face full of black soot
Talkin' at the heat put
Plants in the bed but
The phone's tapped anyway
Maggie says that many say
They must bust in early Man
Orders from the D.A.
Look out kid
Don't matter what you did
Walk on your tip toes
Don't try "No Doz"
Better stay away from those
That carry around a fire hose
Keep a clean nose
Watch the plain clothes
You don't need a weather man
To know which way the wind blows.

Verse 3:
Get sick, get well
Hang around an ink well
Ring bell, hard to tell
If anything is goin' to sell
Try hard, get barred
Get back, write braille
Get jailed, jump bail
Join the army if you fail
Look out kid, you're gonna get hit
But users, cheaters
Six time losers
Hang around the theatres
Girl by the whirlpool
Lookin' for a new fool
Don't follow leaders
Watch the parkin' meters.

Verse 4:
Ah get born, keep warm
Short pants, romance, learn to dance
Get dressed, get blessed
Try to be a success
Please her, please him, buy gifts
Don't steal, don't lift
Twenty years of schoolin'
And they put you on the day shift
Look out kid, they keep it all hid
Better jump down a manhole
Light yourself a candle,
Don't wear sandles
Try to avoid the scandals
Don't wanna be a bum
You better chew gum
The pump don't work
'Cause the vandals took the handles.

I SAY A LITTLE PRAYER

Words by Hal David
Music by Burt Bacharach

Medium tempo

Lyrics:

1.The mo - ment I wake up

(Verse 2 see block lyric)

be - fore I put on my make - up I say a lit - tle prayer for you.

While comb - ing my hair now

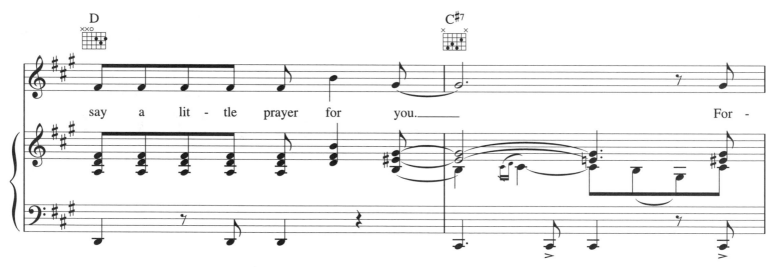

and won - d'ring what dress to wear now._____ I

say a lit - tle prayer for you._____ For -

ev - er, for - ev - er you'll stay in my heart_____ and I will love you for -

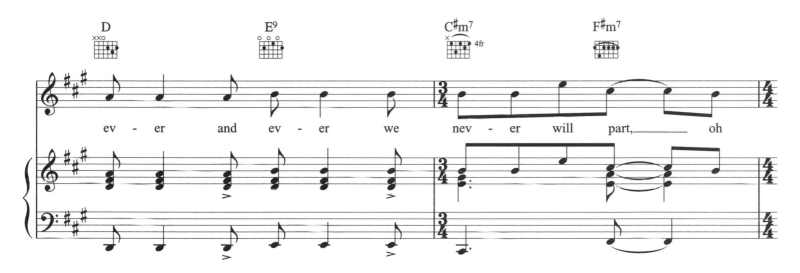

ev - er and ev - er we nev - er will part, _____ oh

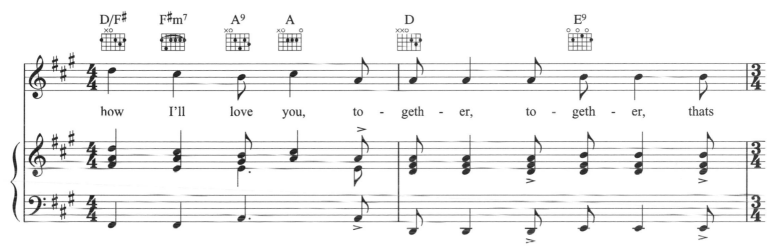

how I'll love you, to - geth - er, to - geth - er, thats

how it must be. _____ To live with - out you would

1. Smoothly

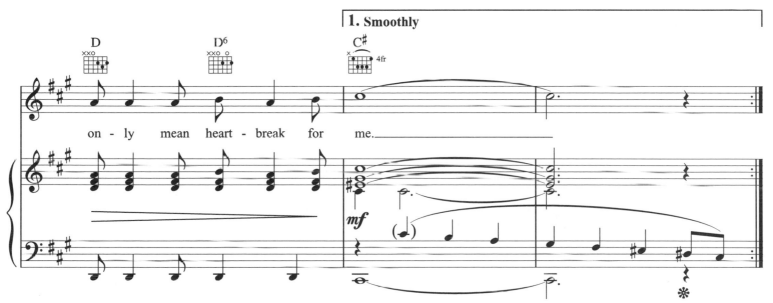

on - ly mean heart - break for me. _____

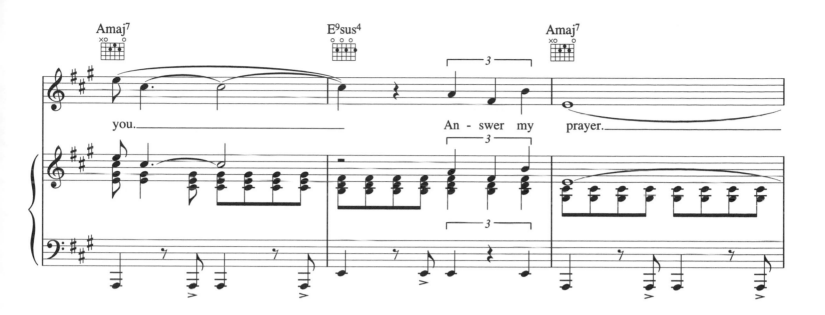

Verse 2:
I run for the bus, dear.
While riding, I think of us dear.
I say a little prayer for you.
At work I just take time,
And all through my coffee break time
I say a little prayer for you.

FOR ONCE IN MY LIFE

Words by Ronald Miller
Music by Orlando Murden

SEX MACHINE (PART 1)

Words & Music by James Brown, Bobby Byrd & Ronald Lenhoff

use your form _ Stay on the scene like a

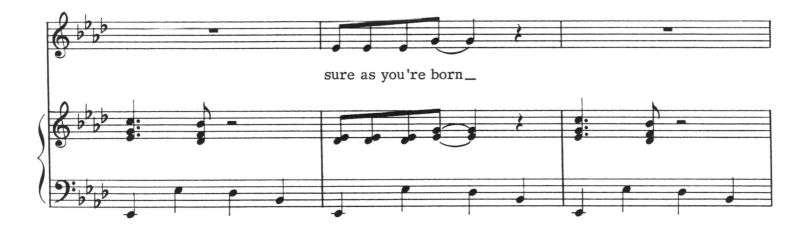

sex ma-chine. _ You got to have the feel - ing

sure as you're born _

Get it to-geth - er right on, _ right on. _

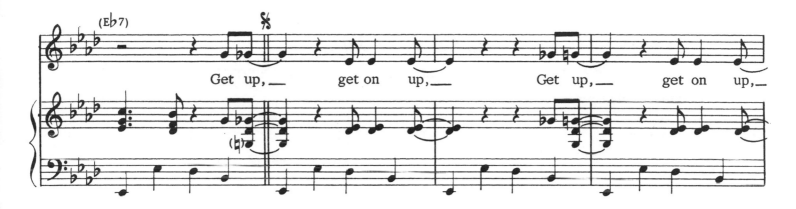

Get up,__ get on up,__ Get up,__ get on up,__

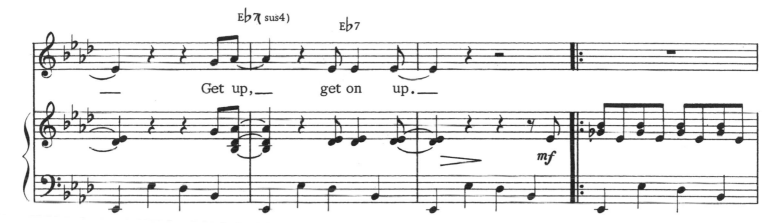

Get up,__ get on up.__

Get up__

ADDITIONAL WORDS:
I said the feeling you got to get,
Give me the fever in a cold sweat.
The way I like it is the way it is;
I got mine and don't worry 'bout his.

Get on up and then shake your money maker,
Shake your money maker, etc.

BABY LOVE

Words & Music by Brian Holland, Eddie Holland & Lamont Dozier

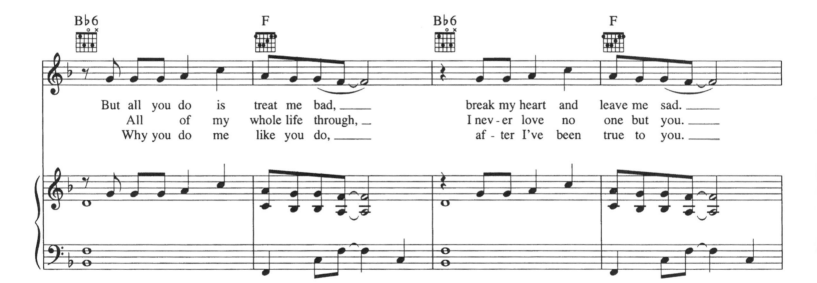

Ba-by love, my ba-by love, been miss-ing ya, miss _ kiss-ing ya. In - stead of
hold you once a - gain my love, feel your warm _ em - brace my love. Don't throw our

break-ing up, _ let's start some kiss-ing and mak-ing up. _ Don't throw our
love a - way, _ please don't do me this way. _ Not hap-py like I

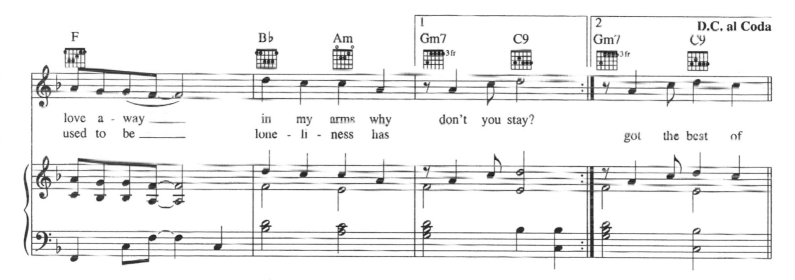

love a - way _ in my arms why don't you stay?
used to be _ lone - li - ness has got the best of

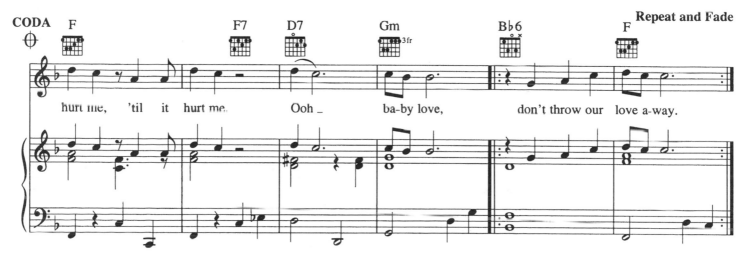

hurt me, 'til it hurt me. Ooh _ ba-by love, don't throw our love a-way.

79

(YOU GOTTA) FIGHT
FOR YOUR RIGHT (TO PARTY)

Words & Music by Rick Rubin, Adam Yauch & Adam Horovitz

Original Key: G#m

♩ = 130

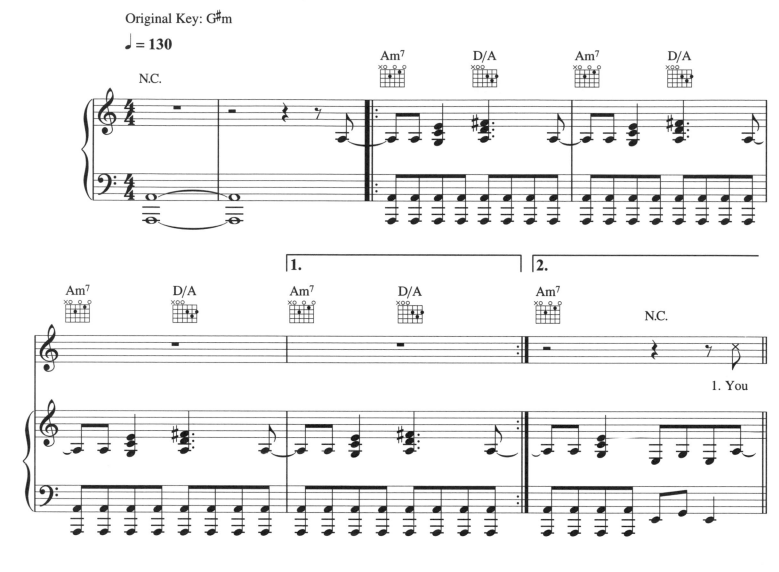

wake up late for school, man, you don't wan-na go.
(2.) pop's caught you smoking and he says, "no___ way".
(3.) out of this___ house if that's the clothes you're gon-na wear.

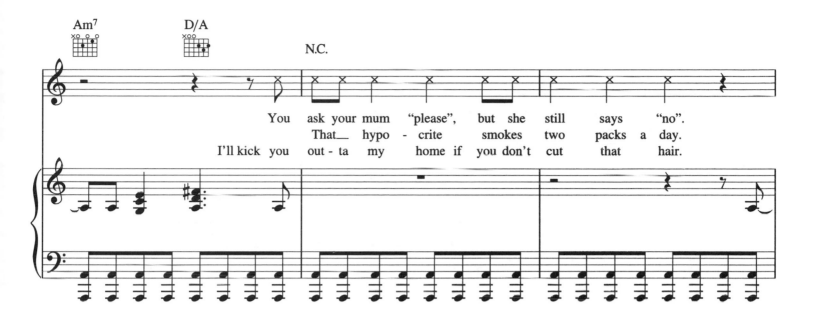

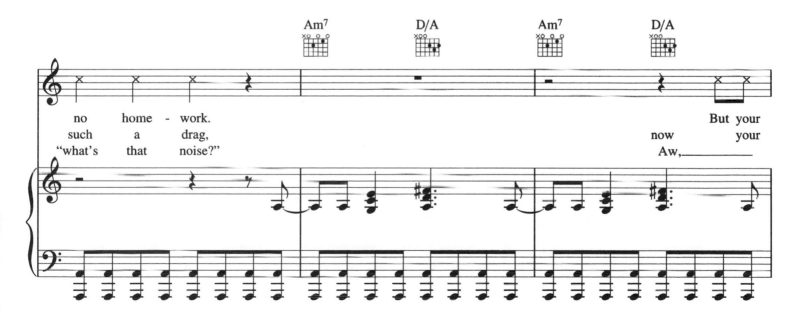

You got - ta fight.

Guitar solo

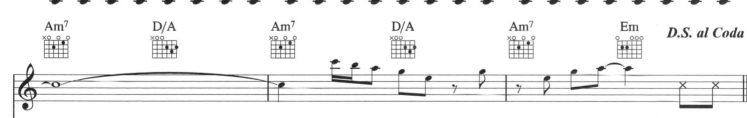

D.S. al Coda

3. Don't step

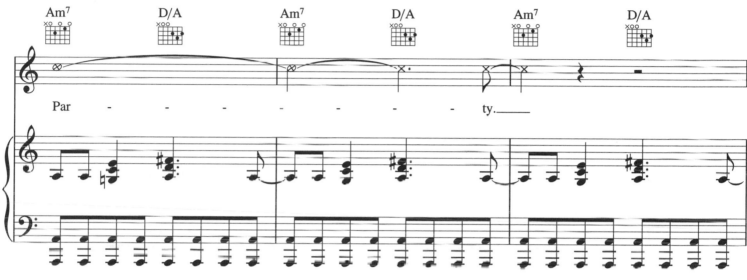

Par - - - - - - ty.____

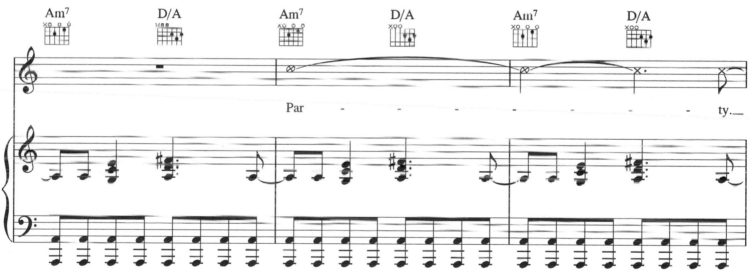

Par - - - - - - - ty.__

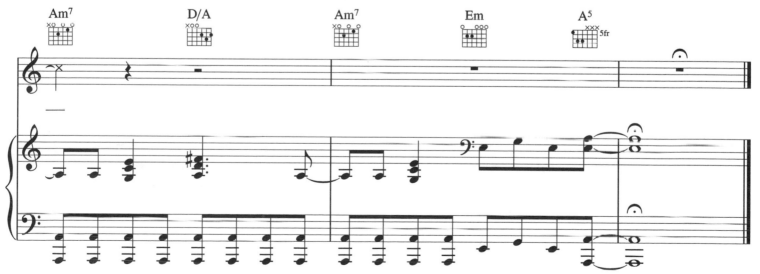

DON'T BELIEVE THE HYPE

Words & Music by Carlton Ridenhour, Eric Sadler & Hank Shocklee

(Don't don't don't don't don't don't don't.)

Back, caught you look-in' for the same thing, it's a new thing, check out this__ I bring.

Uh oh the roll be-low the le-vel 'cause I'm liv-in' low, next to the bass. (Come on,)__ turn up the ra-di-o.

Don't, don't don't don't don't be - lieve___ the hype.)

Repeat ad lib.

Verse 3 see block lyric

(Don't be - lieve, don't don't don't be - lieve___ the hype.

Don't be - lieve, don't don't don't be - lieve___ the hype.) I got

90

91

Verse 2:
Yes
Was the start of my last jam
So here it is again, another def jam
But since I gave you all a little something
That I knew you lacked
They still consider me a new jack.
All the critics you can hang 'em
I'll hold the rope
But they hope to the Pope
And pray it ain't dope
The follower of Farrakhan
Don't tell me that you understand
Until you hear the man.
The book of the new school rap game
Writers treat me like Coltrane, insane
Yes to them, but to me I'm a different kind
We're brothers of the same mind, unblind
Caught in the middle and
Not surrenderin'
I don't rhyme for the sake of riddlin'
Some claim that I'm a smuggler
Some say I never heard of ya
A rap burgler, false media
We don't need it do we?
(It's fake that's what it be to ya, dig me?
Yo, Terminator X, step up on the stand
And show these people what time it is boy.)
Don't believe the hype..*etc*..

Verse 3:
Don't believe the hype - it's a sequel
As an equal, can I get this through to you?
My 98's boomin' with a trunk of funk
All the jealous punks can't stop the dunk.
Comin' from the school of hard knocks
Some perpetrate, they drink Clorox
Attack the black, cause I know they lack exact
The cold facts, and still they try to Xerox.
The leader of the new school, uncool
Never played the fool, just made the rules
Remember there's a need to get alarmed
Again I said I was a timebomb.
In the daytime radio's scared of me
'Cause I'm mad, plus I'm the enemy
They can't c'mon and play with me in primetime
'Cause I know the time, plus I'm gettin' mine.
I get on the mix late in the night
They know I'm livin' right, so here go the mike, sike
Before I let it go, don't rush my show
You try to reach and grab and get elbowed.
Word to Herb, yo if you can't swing this
Learn the words, you might sing this
Just a little bit of the taste of the bass for you
As you get up and dance at the LQ.

cont.
When some deny it, defy if I swing bolos
Then they clear the lane I go solo
The meaning of all of that
Some media is the whack
As you believe it's true, it blows me through the roof
Suckers, liars get me a shovel
Some writers I know are damn devils
From them I say don't believe the hype
(Yo Chuck, they must be on a pipe, right?)
Their pens and pads I'll snatch
'Cause I've had it
I'm not an addict fiendin' for static
I'll see their tape recorder and I grab it
(No, you can't have it back silly rabbit.)
I'm going' to my media assassin
Harry Allen, I gotta ask him
(Yo Harry, you're a writer, are we that type?)
(Don't believe the hype.
Now here's what I want you all to do for me)
Don't believe the hype..*etc*..

Verse 4:
I got flava and all those things you know
(Yeah boy, part two bum rush this show
Yo Griff!) Get the green, black, and red and
Gold down, countdown to Armageddon
-88 you wait the S1s will
Put the let in effect and I still will
Rock the hard jams - treat it like a seminar
Reach the bourgeoise, and rock the boulevard
Some say I'm negative
But they're not positive
But what I got to give...
Red, black and green, y'know what I mean?
(The media says this?)
Yo, don't believe that hype,
They gotta be ringin' that pipe
Ya know what I'm sayin'?
Yo, the mega's got them going up to see
Captain Kirk, like the jerk they're outta work.
Lemme tell you a little something man:
A lot of people on daytime radio are scared of us
Because they're too ignorant to understand
The lyrics of the truth that we publish,
And I'm proud that I've got brain cells.
They just puttin' down the words and 'stead they call
Cabs, d'you know what I'm sayin'?
But their heads are s'posed to straighten
It out - quick, fast, in a hurry.
Don't worry, flava - vision ain't blurry,
D'you know what I'm sayin'?
Yo - Terminator X!)
Don't believe the hype..*etc*..

WOMAN

Words & Music by John Lennon

doo doo. Wo - man, please let me ex - plain.

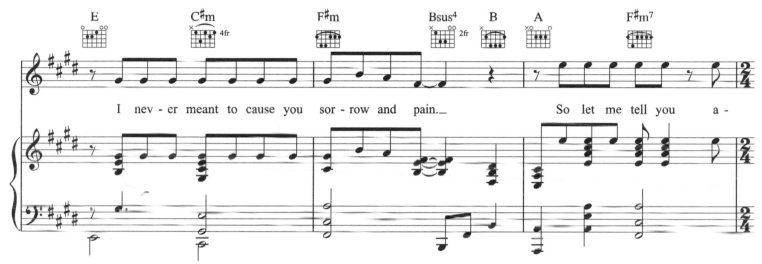

I nev - er meant to cause you sor - row and pain. So let me tell you a -

-gain and a - gain and a - gain. I

love_____ you, yeah, yeah, now and for - ev - er. I

Repeat to fade

FIRESTARTER

Words & Music by Liam Howlett, Keith Flint, Kim Deal, Trevor Horn,
Anne Dudley, Jonathan Jeczalik, Paul Morley & Gary Langan

1. I'm the trou-ble start-er,   punk-in' in-sti-ga - tor.
2. I'm the bitch you ha-ted,   filth in-fa-tu-a - ted.   Yeah.
3. I'm the self in-flict-ed   punk de-to-na - tor.   Yeah.

I'm the fear ad-dic - ted, dan - ger il - lus - tra - ted.
I'm the pain you tas - ted, fell in - tox - i - ca - ted.
I'm the one in - ven - ted twist-ed a - ni - ma - tor.

I'm a fi-re - start - er, t - wist-ed fi-re - start - er.

You're the fi-re - start - er, twist-ed fi-re - start - er.

To Coda ⊕ | 1.

I'm a fi-re - start - er, twist-ed fi-re - start - er.

D.S. al Coda

⊕ Coda

I'm a fi-re-start-er,   twist-ed fi-re-start-er.

F#m⁷

N.C.

NO WOMAN, NO CRY

Words & Music by Vincent Ford

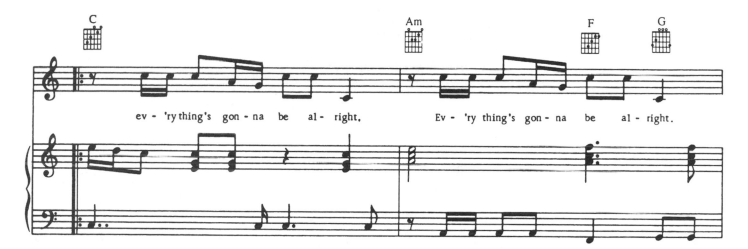

ev - 'ry thing's gon - na be al - right,   Ev - 'ry thing's gon - na be al - right.

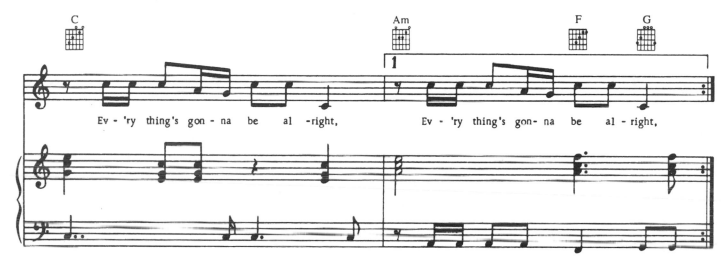

Ev - 'ry thing's gon - na be al - right,   Ev - 'ry thing's gon - na be al - right,

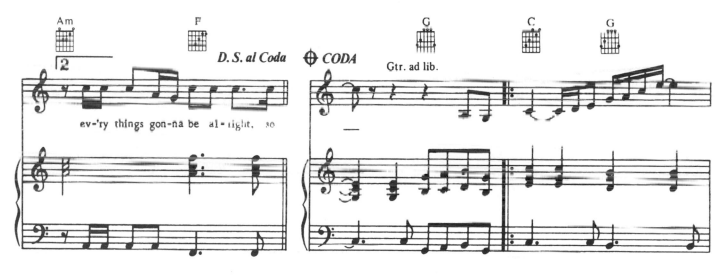

D.S. al Coda   CODA   Gtr. ad lib.

ev - 'ry things gon - na be al - right, so

To fade

LIFE ON MARS?

Words & Music by David Bowie

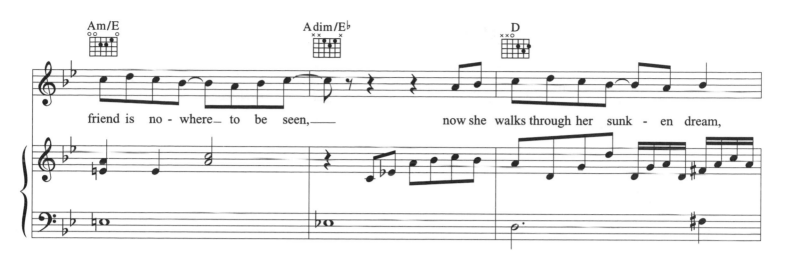

friend is no - where_ to be seen,___ now she walks through her sunk - en dream,

to the seat with the clear - est view and she's

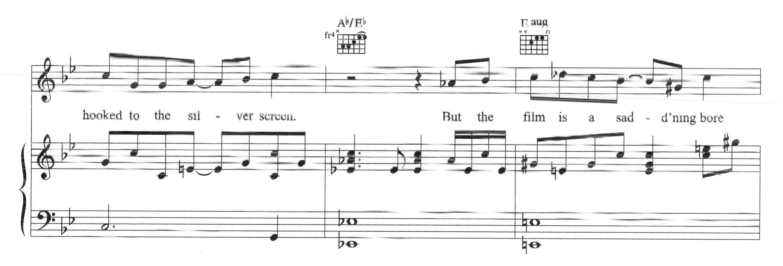

hooked to the sil - ver screen. But the film is a sad - d'ning bore

for she's lived it ten times_ or more. She could

spit in the eyes___ of fools___ as they ask her to fo - cus on

sail - ors fight - ing in the dance hall. Oh man,

look at those cave - men go, it's the freak - i - est show.

Take a look at the law - man

beat - ing up the wrong guy. Oh, man, won - der if he'll ev - er know

he's in the best sell - ing show.

Is there life___ on Mars?

To Coda ⊕

Verse 2:
It's on Amerika's tortured brow that Mickey Mouse has grown up a cow
Now the workers have struck for fame 'cause Lennon's on sale again
See the mice in their million hordes, from Ibiza to the Norfolk Broads
Rule Brittania is out of bounds to my mother, my dog and clowns
But the film is a saddening bore 'cause I wrote it ten times or more
It's about to be writ again as I ask her to focus on

Sailors fighting in the dance hall *etc.*

DON'T LOOK BACK IN ANGER

Words & Music by Noel Gallagher

1. Slip in-side___ the eye of your mind,___ don't you know you might___ find___
(Verse 2 see block lyric)

a bet-ter place to play.___

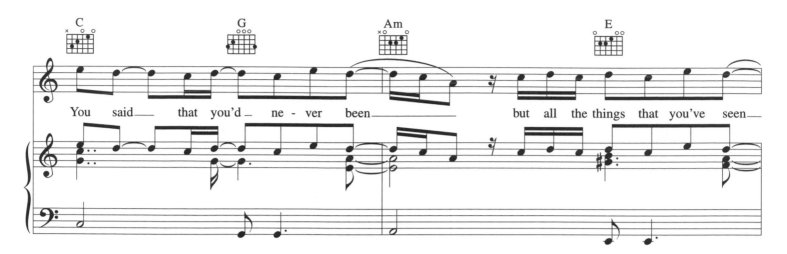

You said — that you'd — ne - ver been — but all the things that you've seen —

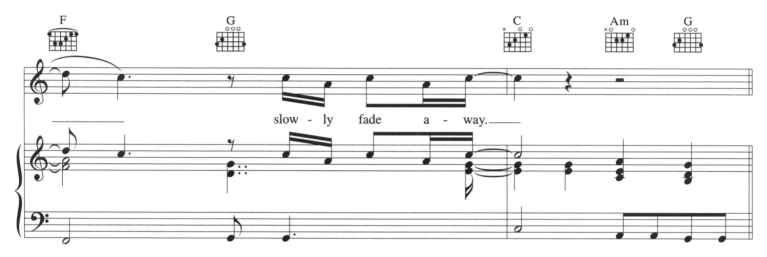

— slow - ly fade a - way. —

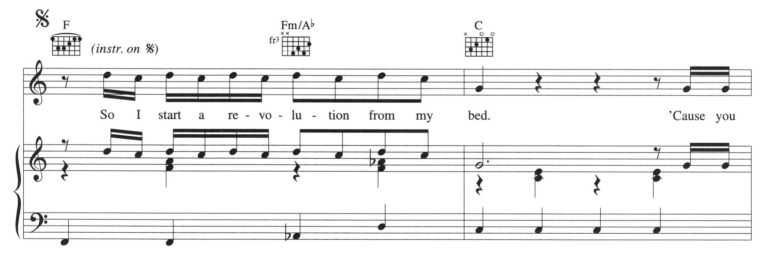

So I start a re - vo - lu - tion from my bed. 'Cause you

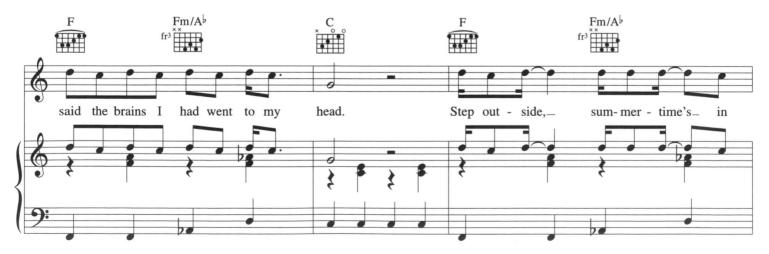

said the brains I had went to my head. Step out - side, — sum - mer - time's — in

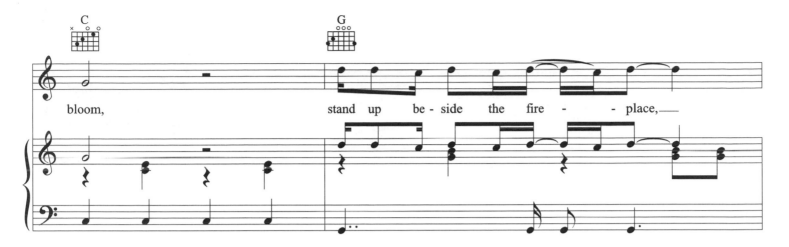

bloom,   stand up be - side the fire - - place, ____

take that look from off ____ your face, ____ you ain't ev - er gon - na burn ____ my ____

____ heart ____ out ____

So   Sal - ly can wait ____ she knows it's too late ____ as {we're / she's} walk - ing on by ____

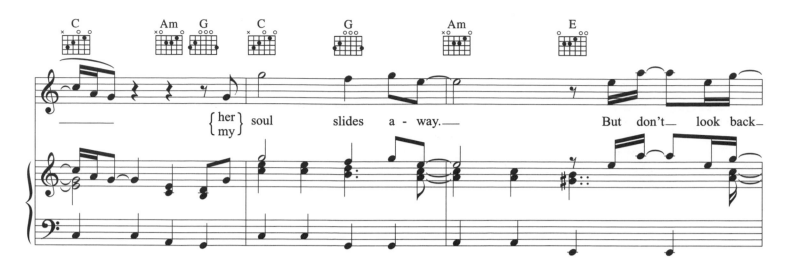

{her / my} soul slides a - way.___ But don't___ look back___

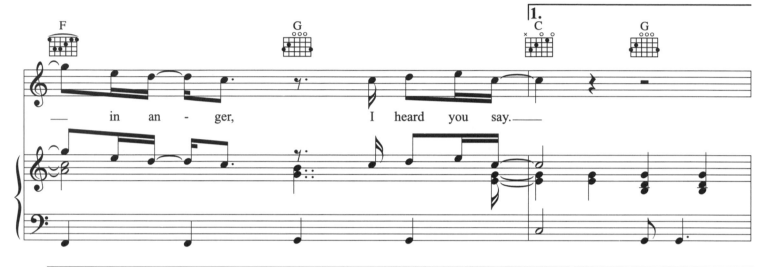

__ in an - ger, I heard you say.___

1.

2, 3. ***D.S. al Coda***
To Coda ⊕

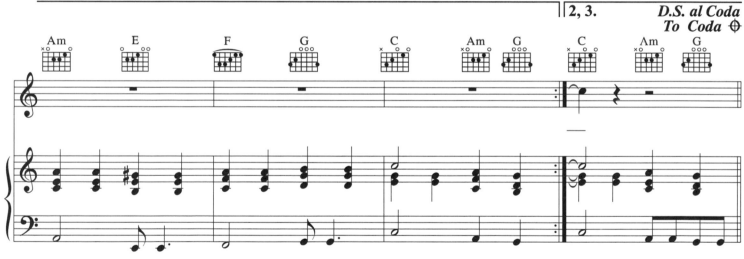

⊕ ***Coda***

So Sal - ly can wait___ she knows it's too late___ as she's walk - ing on by___

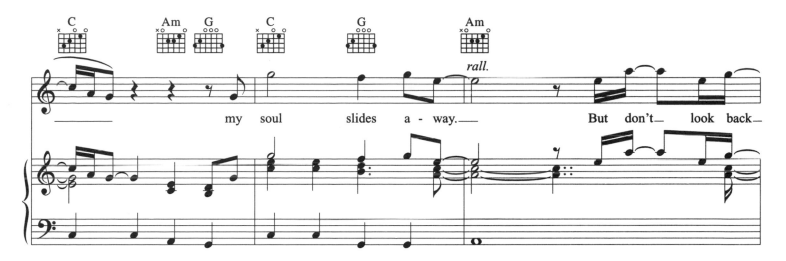

my soul slides a - way.___ But don't___ look back___

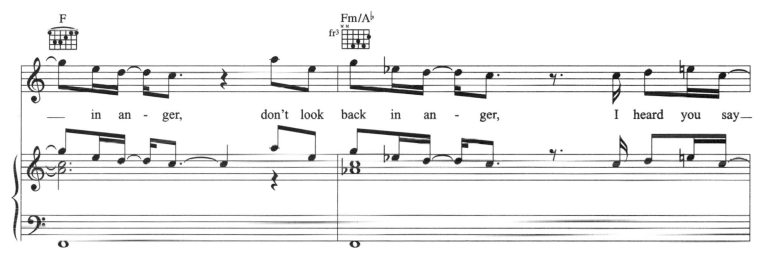

___ in an - ger, don't look back in an - ger, I heard you say___

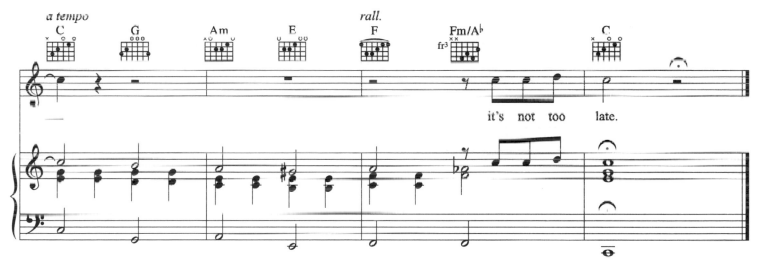

it's not too late.

Verse 2:
Take me to the place where you go
Where nobody knows if it's night or day
Please don't put your life in the hands
Of a rock 'n' roll band who'll throw it all away.

I'm gonna start a revolution from my head
'Cause you said the brains I had went to my head
Step outside, the summertime's in bloom
Stand up beside the fireplace, take that look from off your face
'Cause you ain't never gonna burn my heart out.

PARANOID ANDROID

Words & Music by Thom Yorke, Jonny Greenwood,
Colin Greenwood, Ed O'Brien & Phil Selway

1. Please could you stop the noise, I'm trying to get some rest
2. When I am King you will be first a - gainst the wall,

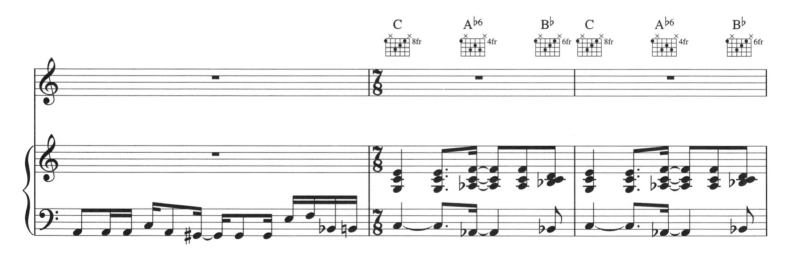

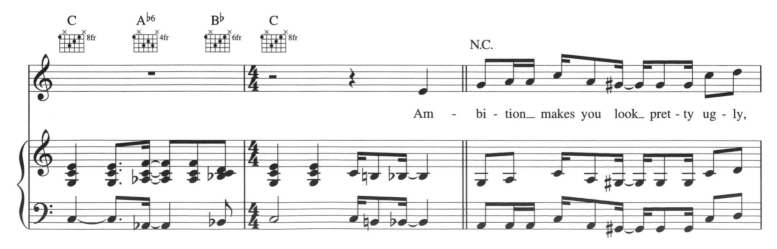

Am - bi - tion_ makes you look_ pret - ty ug - ly,

kick - ing and squeal-ing Guc - ci lit - tle pig - gy.

You don't re - mem - ber. you don't re - mem - ber,

why don't you re-mem-ber my name?_ Off with his head,_ man, off_ with his head, man.

Why don't you re-mem-ber my name?_ I guess_ he does..._____

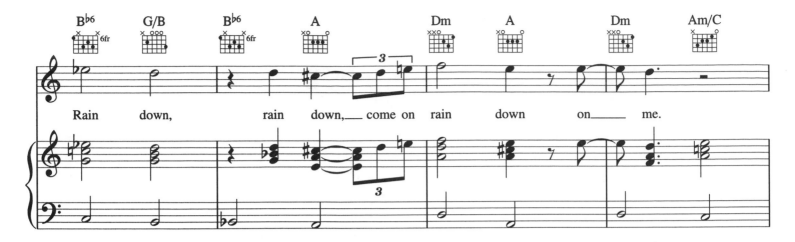

Rain down, rain down, come on rain down on me.

From a great height, from a great height, height.

Rain down, rain down, come on rain down on me.

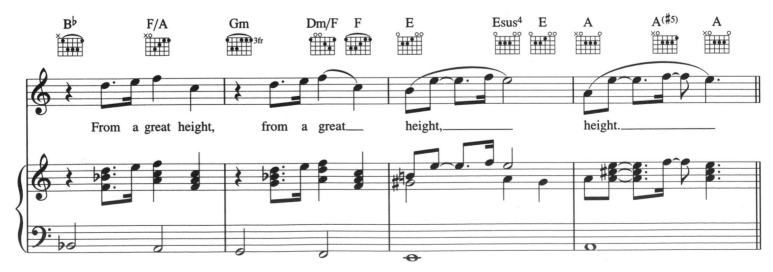

From a great height, from a great height, height.

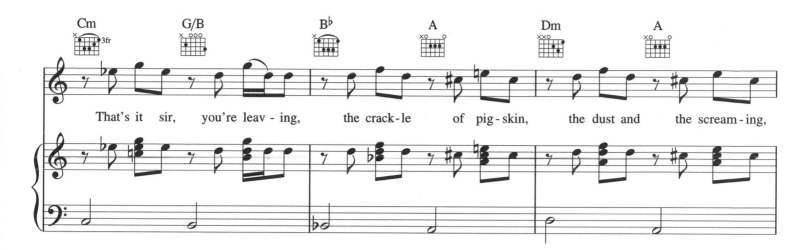

That's it sir, you're leav-ing, the crack-le of pig-skin, the dust and the scream-ing,

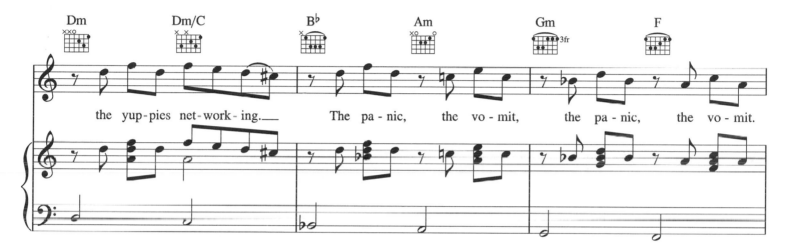

the yup-pies net-work-ing.___ The pa-nic, the vo-mit, the pa-nic, the vo-mit.

God loves his child-ren, God loves his child-ren, yeah.

Tempo primo

N.C.

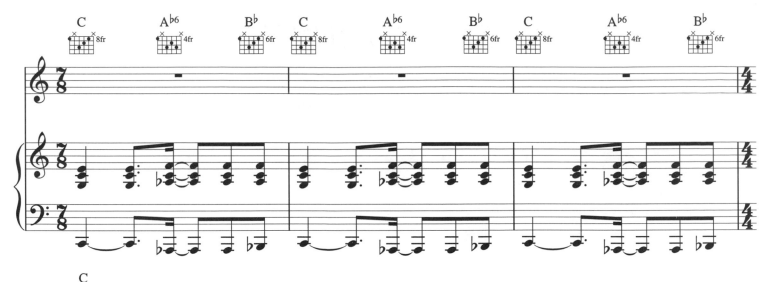

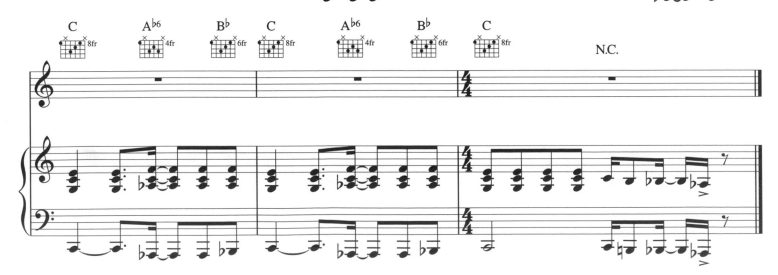

WATERLOO SUNSET

Words & Music by Ray Davies

1. Dir-ty old riv-er must you keep roll-ing, flow-ing in-to__

(Verses 2 & 3 see block lyric)

__ the night. Peo-ple so bu-sy, make me feel diz-zy, ta-xi lights shine__

so bright. But I don't_____ need no friends.__

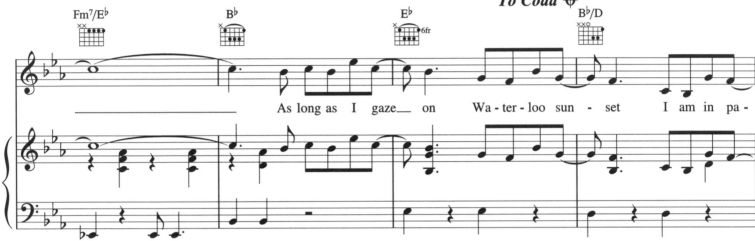

To Coda ⊕

_____ As long as I gaze__ on Wa-ter-loo sun-set I am in pa-

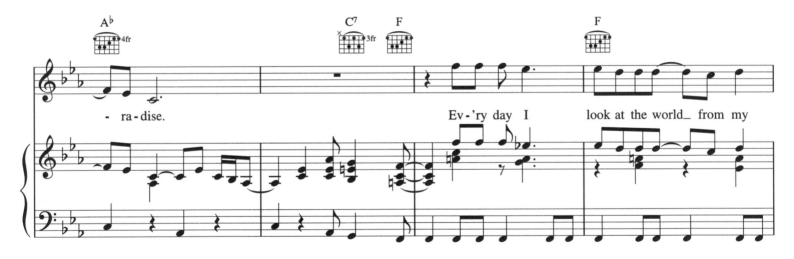

-ra-dise. Ev-'ry day I look at the world__ from my

win-dow. The chil-ly, chil-li-est eve-ning time.__

Verse 2:
Terry met Julie, Waterloo Station, every Friday night.
But I am so lazy, don't want to wander, I stay at home at night.
But I don't feel afraid.
As long as I gaze on Waterloo sunset I am in paradise.

Ev'ry day I look at the world *etc.*

Verse 3:
Millions of people swarming like flies round Waterloo underground.
Terry and Julie lie cross over the river where they feel safe and sound.
And they don't need no friends.
As long as they gaze on Waterloo sunset they are in paradise.

Ev'ry day I look at the world *etc.*

HOW SOON IS NOW?

Words & Music by Morrissey & Johnny Marr

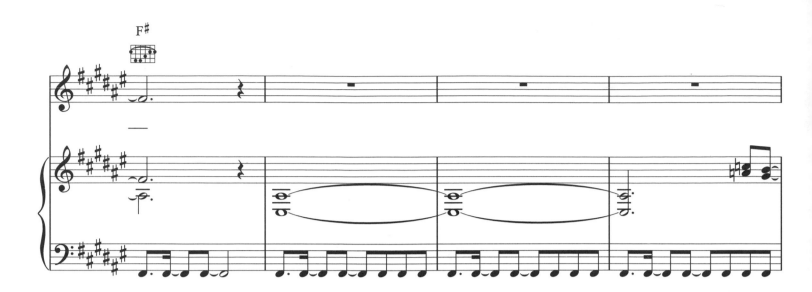

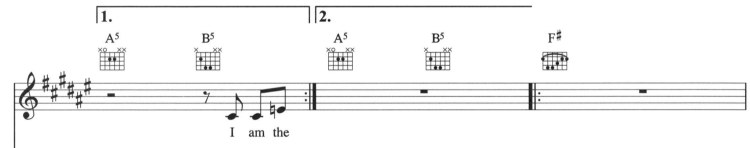

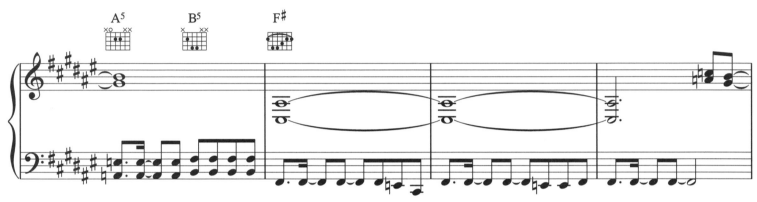

I am the

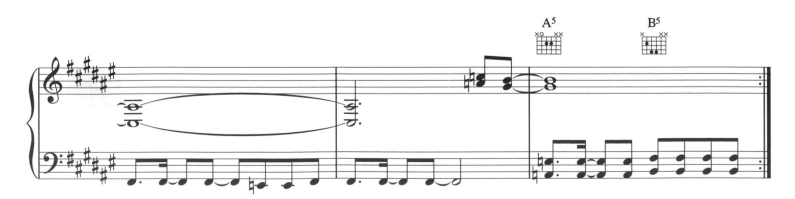

LONDON CALLING

Words & Music by Joe Strummer, Mick Jones, Paul Simonon & Topper Headon

♩ = 132 (swung quavers)

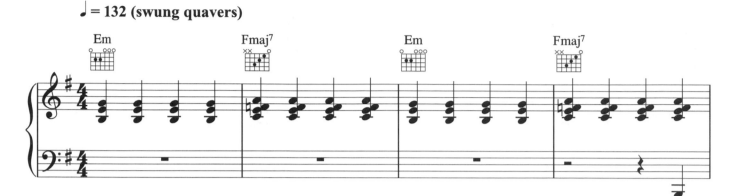

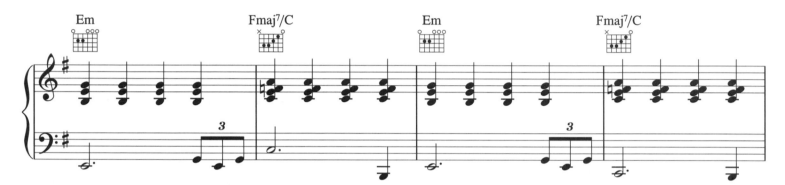

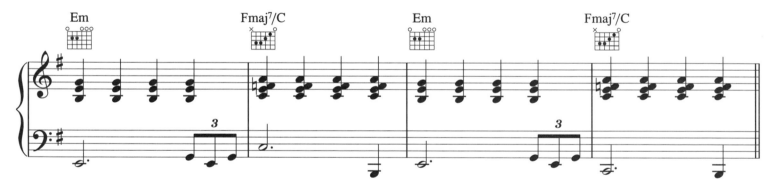

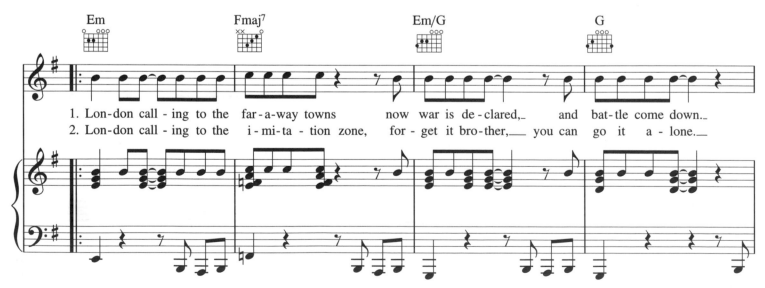

1. Lon-don call-ing to the far-a-way towns   now war is de-clared,__   and bat-tle come down.__
2. Lon-don call-ing to the i-mi-ta-tion zone,   for-get it bro-ther,__ you can go it a-lone.__

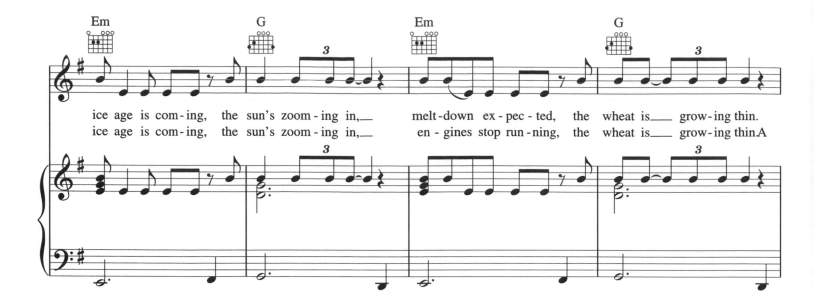

ice age is com-ing, the sun's zoom-ing in,___ melt-down ex-pec-ted, the wheat is___ grow-ing thin.
ice age is com-ing, the sun's zoom-ing in,___ en-gines stop run-ning, the wheat is___ grow-ing thin.A

En-gines stop run-ning, but I have no fear 'cause Lon-don is drown-ing, I___
nu-cle-ar er-ror, but I have no fear, 'cause Lon-don is drown-ing, and

live by the riv-er. I, I live by the riv-er.___

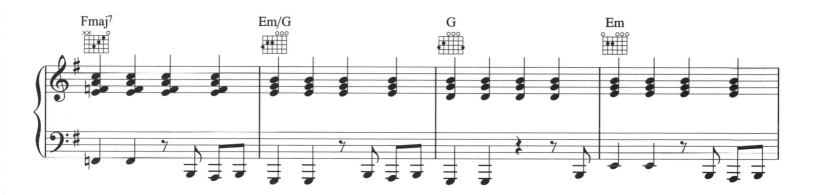

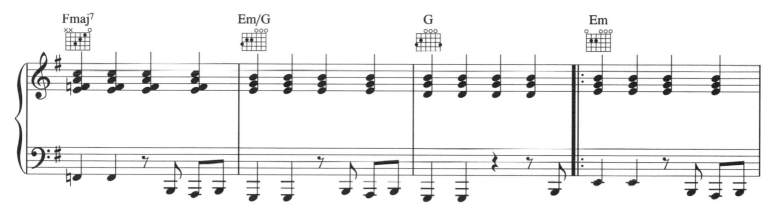

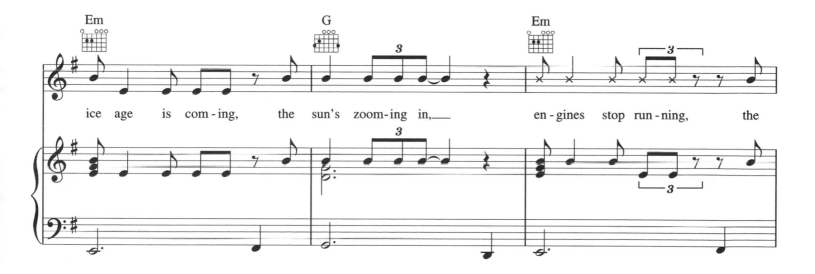

ice age is com-ing, the sun's zoom-ing in,___ en-gines stop run-ning, the

133

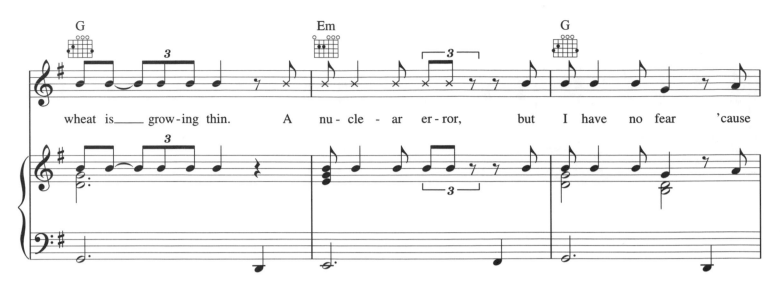

wheat is___ grow-ing thin. A nu – cle – ar er – ror, but I have no fear 'cause

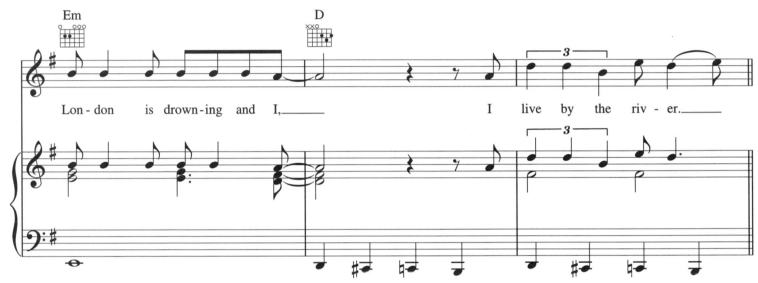

Lon – don is drown-ing and I,___ I live by the riv – er.___

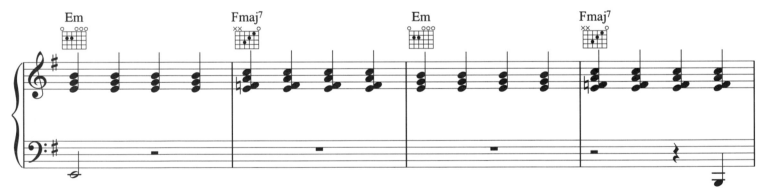

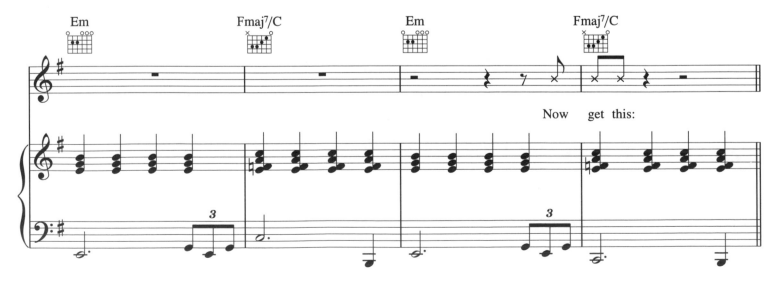

Now get this:

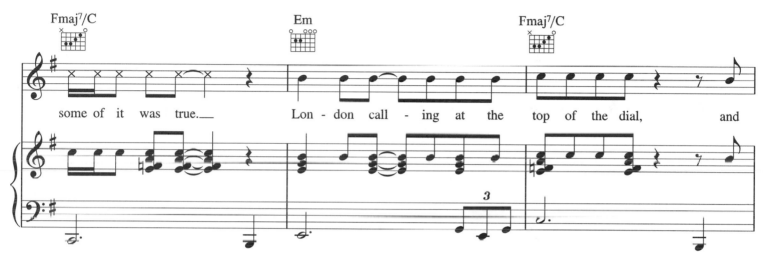

GOOD VIBRATIONS

Words & Music by Brian Wilson & Mike Love

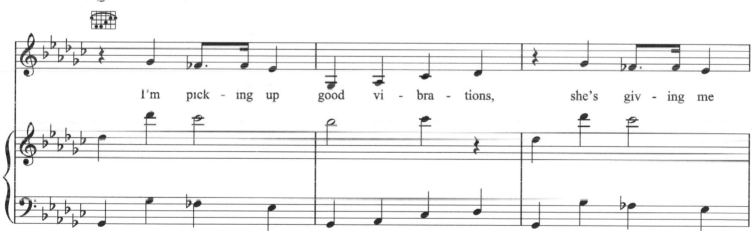

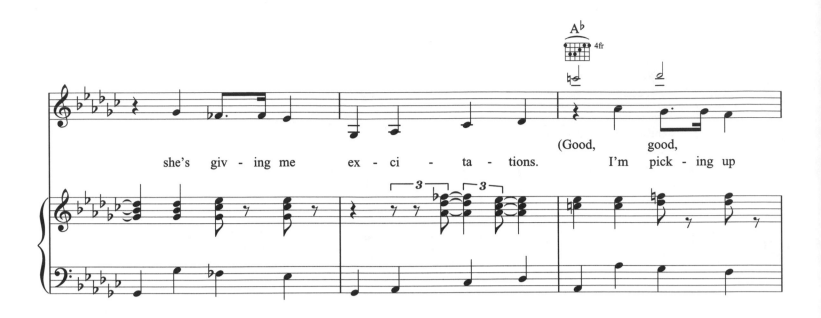

(Good, good,
she's giv - ing me ex - ci - ta - tions. I'm pick - ing up

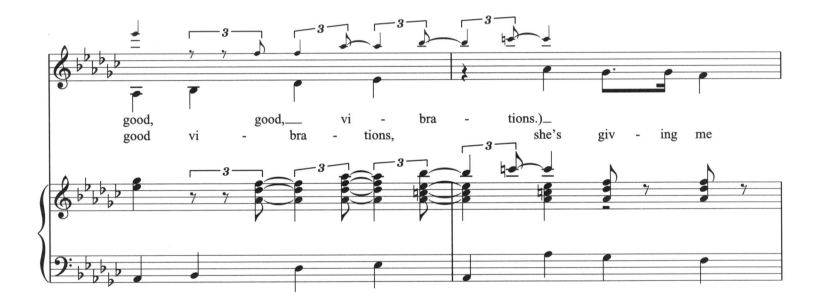

good, good, vi - bra - tions.)
good vi - bra - tions, she's giv - ing me

Good, good, good good vi - bra -
ex - ci - ta - tions. I'm pick - ing up good vi - bra - tions,

138

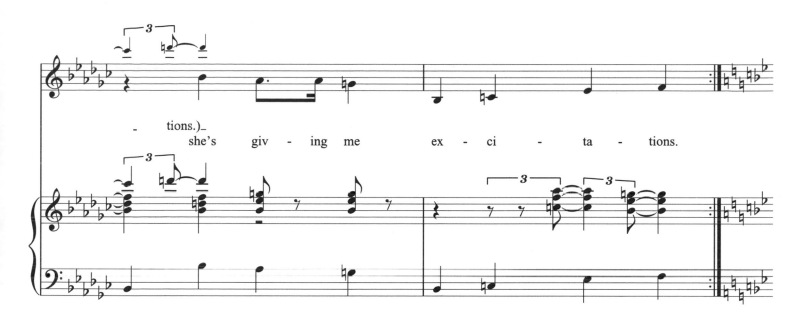

tions.)_ she's giv - ing me ex - ci - ta - tions.

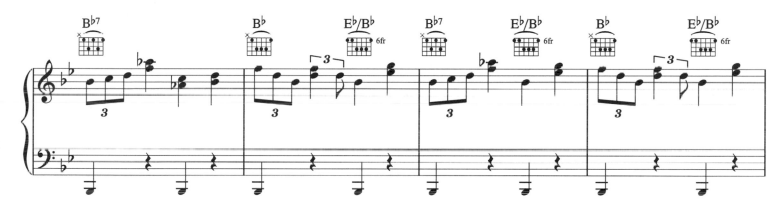

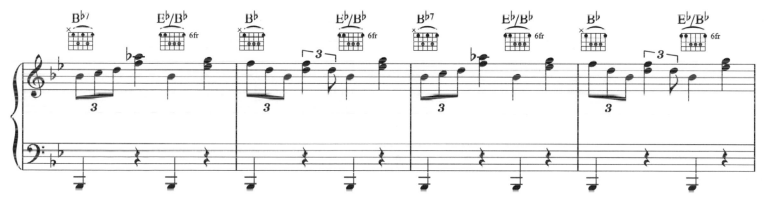

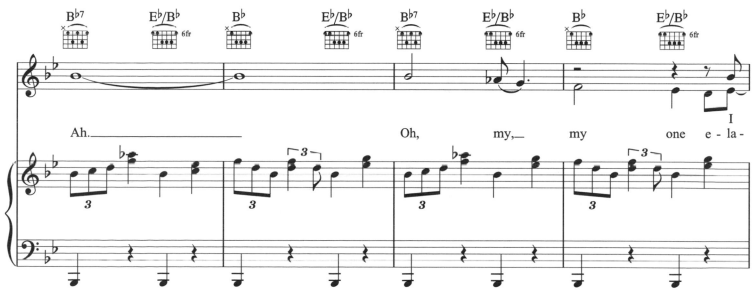

Ah._____ Oh, my,_ my one e - la- I

vi - bra - tions a - happen - in' with her.___ Got - ta keep___ those lov - in' good

vi - bra - tions a - happen - in' with her.___ Got - ta keep___ those lov - in' good

Vocal fades out

vi - bra - tions a - hap...

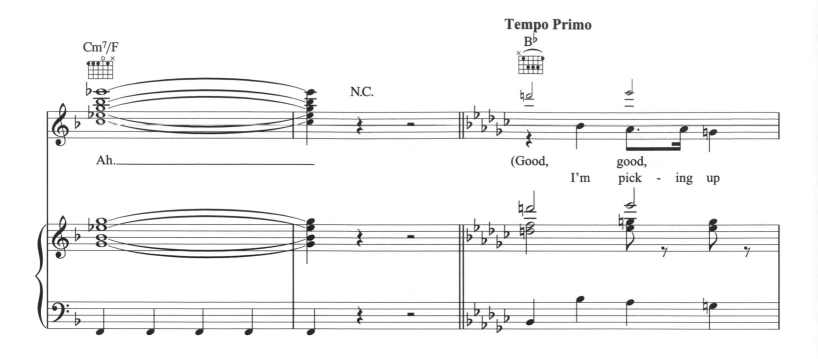

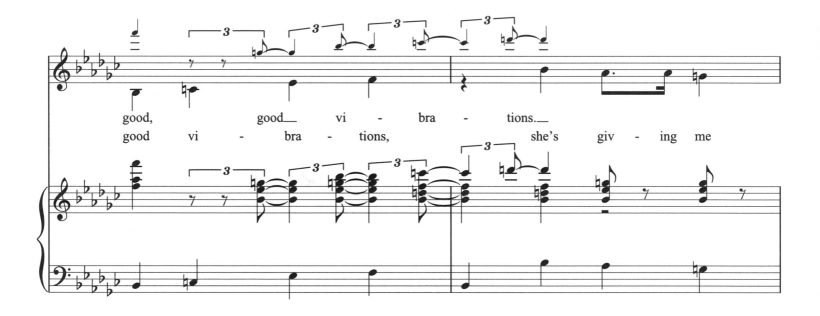

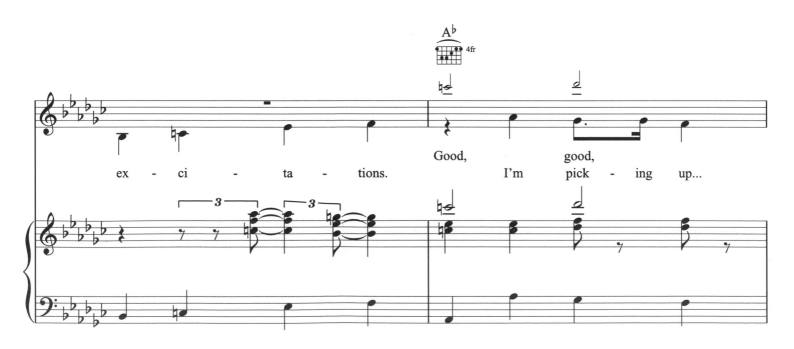

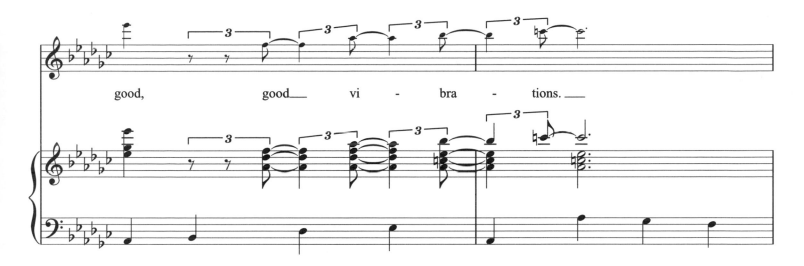

good,   good___ vi - bra - tions. ___

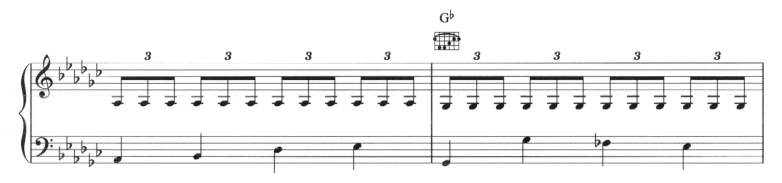

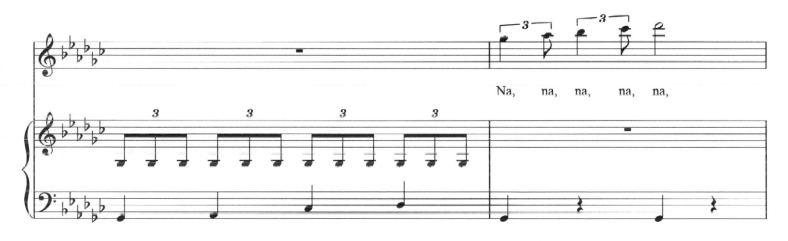

Na, na, na, na, na,

na, na, na.   Na, na, na, na, na,

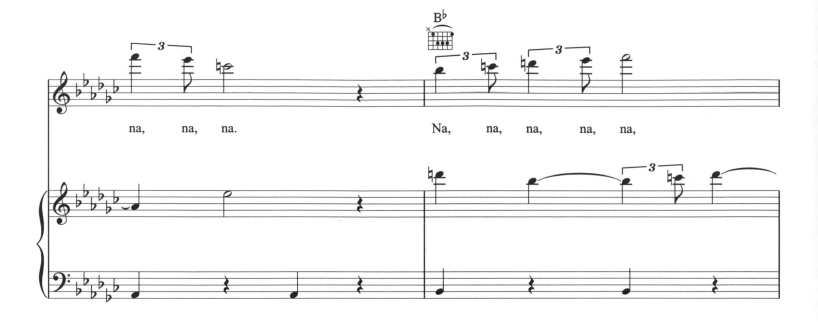

na,   na,   na.   Na,   na,   na,   na,   na,

na,   na,   na.   Na,   na,   na,   na,   na,   na,   na,   na.

Repeat to fade

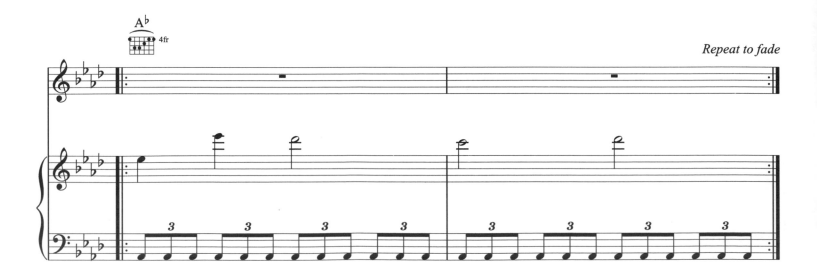

144

Good Golly Miss Molly

Words & Music by Robert Blackwell & John Marascalco

Good Gol - ly Miss Mol - ly,   Yeah you sure like a ball,

Well good gol - ly Miss Mol - ly,   Yeah you sure like a ball.

When you're shak - in' and a shout - in'   Can't you hear your Momma call?

Mom-ma, Pop-pa told me "Son you'd bet-ter watch your step" What I knew a-bout Miss Mol-ly, Got-ta

watch my dad-dy my-self.   Good Gol - ly Miss   Mol - ly

Yeah you sure _ like a ball _____   When you're shak - in' and a

shout - in'   Can't you hear_ your Mom-ma   call?

VENUS IN FURS

Words & Music by Lou Reed

To Coda ⊕

ser - vant, don't for - sake him,
dorn the im - pe - rious,
belt that does a - wait you,

strike, dear mis - tress and cure his heart.
sev - erin, sev - erin a - waits you there.
strike, dear mis - tress and cure his heart.

1.

2.

I am tired,_____

I am wea - ry,

I could sleep for a

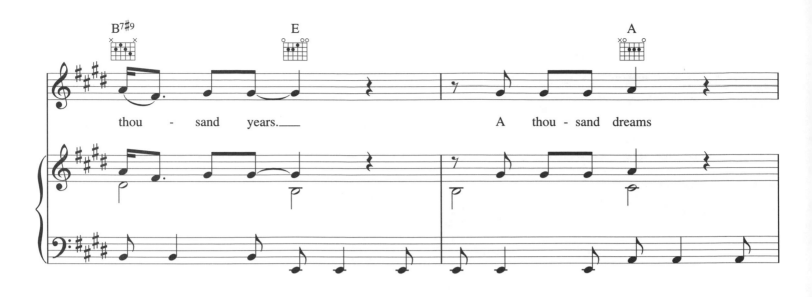

thou - sand years.___ A thou - sand dreams

that would a - wake me,___ diff-'rent co-lours made of tears.

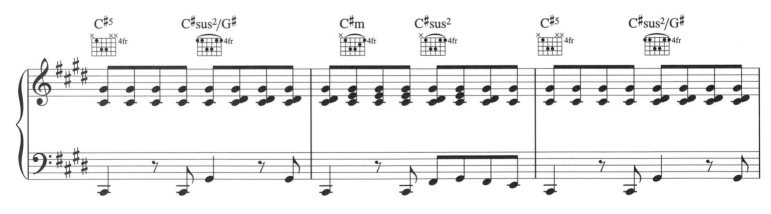

D.S. al Coda

⊕ **Coda**

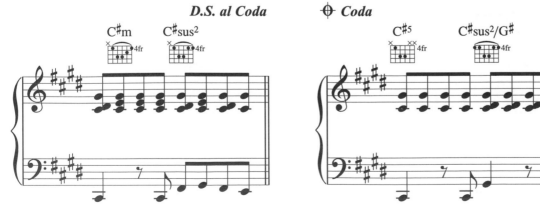

4. Sev-e-rin, sev-e-rin, speak so slight-ly, sev-e-rin down on your

bend-ed knee. Taste the whip, in love not giv-en light-ly,

Taste the whip, now bleed for me.

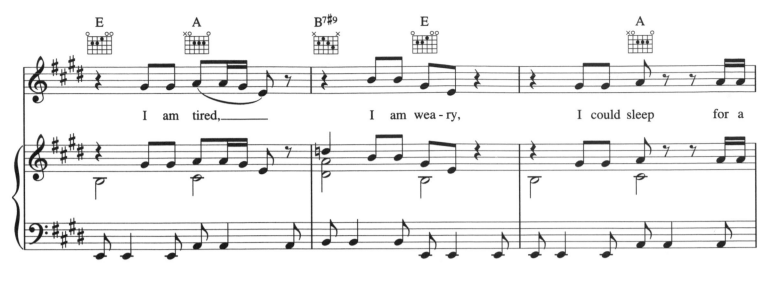

I am tired,_____ I am wea-ry, I could sleep for a

thou - sand years.__ A thou-sand dreams that would a-wake me,

diff-'rent col-ours made of tears.

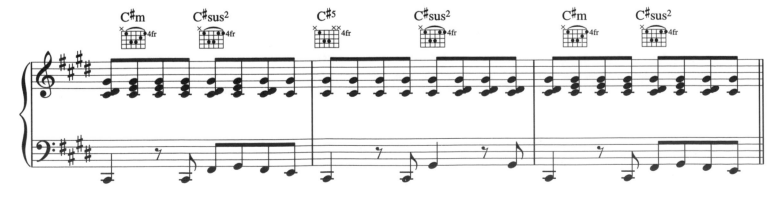

5. Shi - ny, shi - ny, shi - ny boots of lea - ther, whip - lash___ girl - child___ in the dark. Sev - 'rin your ser - vant, comes in bells, please don't for - sake him, strike dear mis - tress and cure his heart.

GOT TO BE THERE

Words & Music by Elliot Willensky

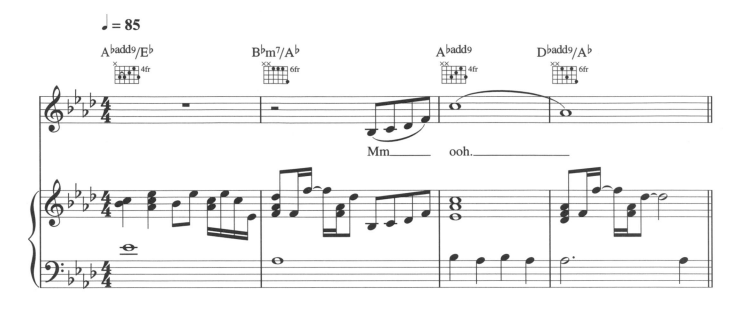

show her that she's my girl.___ Oh,___ what a feel - ing there'll
be___ the mo-ment I___ know she loves me.___
___ 'Cause when I look in her eyes,___ I___ re-a-lise I need her shar-
-ing the world be - side me.___ 2. So I've

I need her shar - ing the world___ be - side me.___

_____ 3. That's why I've

home.___

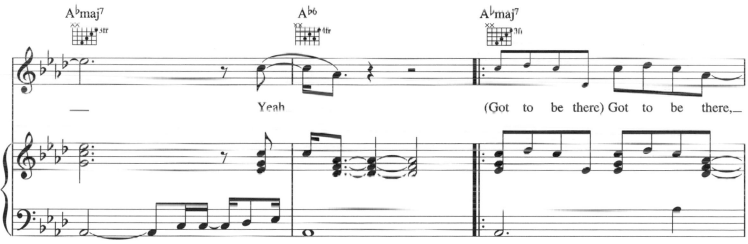

_____ Yeah

(Got to be there) Got to be there,___

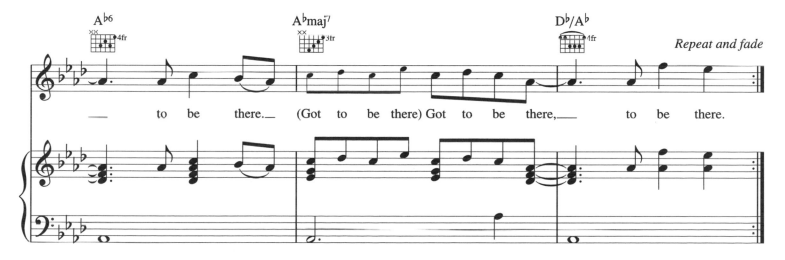

_____ to be there.___ (Got to be there) Got to be there,___ to be there.

Repeat and fade

157

THE YOUNG ONES

Words & Music by Roy Bennett & Sid Tepper

young— ones,_____ darl - ing we're the young— ones._____

(Verses 2-4. see block lyrics)

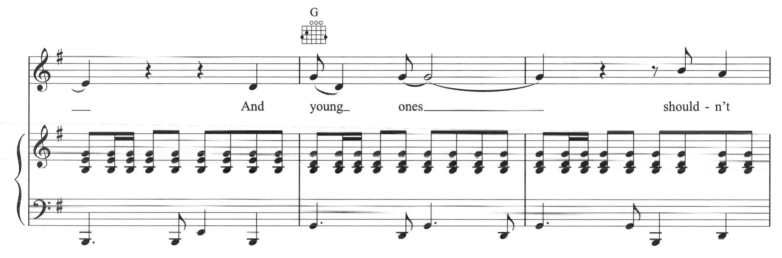

— And young— ones_____ should - n't

bo a - fraid_____ to_____

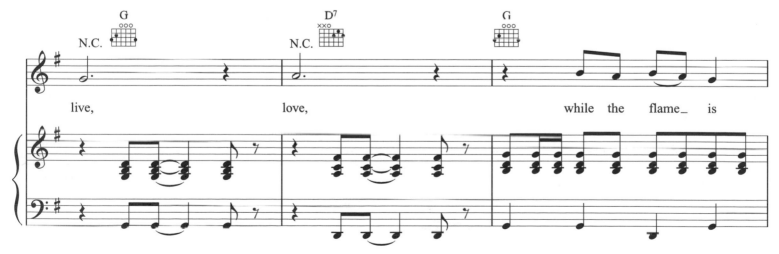

live, love, while the flame— is

strong 'cause we may not be____ the____

young ones ve - ry long.

2. To -

Once in ev - 'ry life - time____

comes a love like_ this.____

Oh, I need_ you and

you need__ me. Oh, my darl - ing can't you see._____

D.%. al Coda I

𝄌 *Coda I*

Guitar

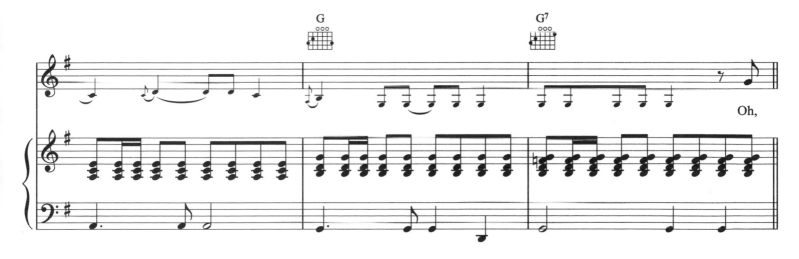

Oh,

once in ev - 'ry life - time_____ comes_

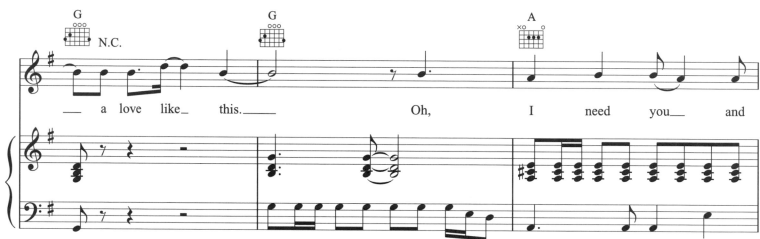

___ a love like_ this.___ Oh, I need you___ and

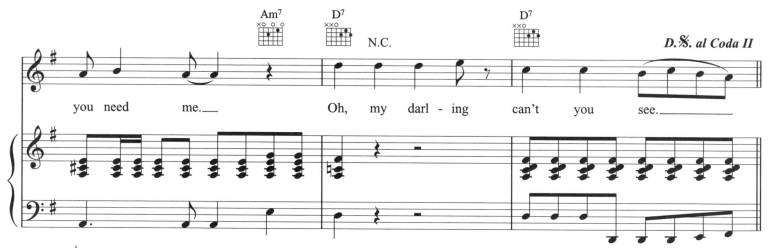

you need me.___ Oh, my darl - ing can't you see.___

D.%. al Coda II

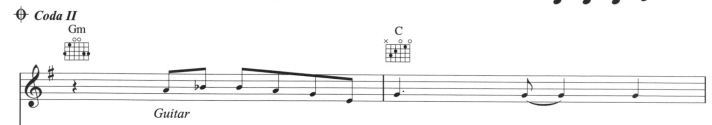

⊕ *Coda II*

Guitar

162

Verse 2:
Tomorrow, why wait until tomorrow?
'Cause tomorrow sometimes never comes
So love me, there's a song to be sung
And the best time is to sing it while we're young.

Verse 3:
Young dreams should be dreamed together
And young hearts shouldn't be afraid
And some day, when the years have flown
Darling, then we'll teach the young ones of our own.

Verse 4 as Verse 3.

PEGGY SUE

Words & Music by Buddy Holly, Norman Petty & Jerry Allison

Oh, well, I love you, gal,___ Yes, I love you, Peg - gy Sue:___

Peg - gy Sue,___

Peg - gy Sue,___ Pret - ty, pret - ty, pret - ty, pret - ty,

Peg - gy Sue,___ Oh, my Peg - gy,___ My

Oh, Peg - gy,_____ My Peg - gy Sue;___

Oh, well, I love you, gal,___

Yes, I want you, Peg - gy Sue.___

JOHNNY B. GOODE

Words & Music by Chuck Berry

Deep down in Lou-'si-an-a, close to New Or-leans,__ Way back up in the woods a-mong the
car-ry his gui-tar__ in a gun-ny sack, Go sit be-neath the tree__ by the
moth-er told him, "Some-day you will be a man__ And you will be the lead-er of a

ev-er - greens;__ There stood an old__ cab-in made of earth and wood,__ Where
rail - road track;__ Ol' en - gineer in the train__ sit-tin' in the shade,__
big old band;__ Man - y peo-ple com-in' from__ miles a - round,__ To

lived a coun-try boy__ named__ John-ny B. Goode.__ Who'd nev-er ev-er learned to read or
Strum-min' with the rhy-thm that the driv-ers made.__ The peo-ple pass-in' by,__ they would
hear you play your mu-sic till the sun goes down.__ May-be some day your name-'ll be in

write so well,___ But he could play a gui - tar___ just like a - ring - in' a bell.___ Go! Go!___
stop and say___ Oh my, but that lit - tle coun - try boy___ could play. Go!
lights___ A - say - in' John - ny B. Goode___ to - night." ___

Go!___ John - ny! Go! Go!___ Go!___ John - ny! Go! Go!___

Go!___ John - ny! Go! Go!___ Go!___ John - ny! Go! Go!___

John - ny B. Goode.___

2. He used to
3. ___ His

PURPLE RAIN

Words & Music by Prince

I nev-er meant 2 cause u ___ a-ny sor-row, -er.

I nev-er meant 2 cause___ u a-ny pain.___
All I wan-na be is some kind of friend.___

I on-ly want-ed one time 2 see u laugh-ing.___
Ba-by I could nev-er steal u from an-oth-er.___ I

on-ly want-ed to see u laugh-ing in the pur-ple rain.}
It's such a shame our friend-ship had 2___ end.} Pur-ple___ rain, pur-ple rain.___

Pur-ple___ rain, pur-ple rain.___

171

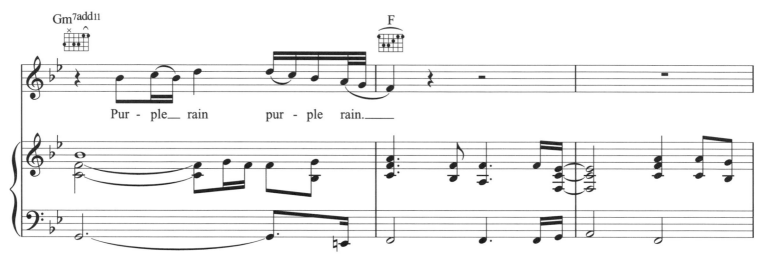

Tacet 1: Ooh   ooh___   ooh___

ooh.   Ooh   ooh___   ooh___   ooh.   Ooh   ooh___   ooh___

ooh.   ooh.

TRAGEDY

Words & Music by Barry Gibb, Maurice Gibb & Robin Gibb

Here I lie in a lost and lone-ly part of town,
Night and day there's a burn-ing down in-side of me.

held in time   in a world of tears   I   slow - ly drown.
Burn - ing love   with a   yearn - ing   that   won't   let   me   be.

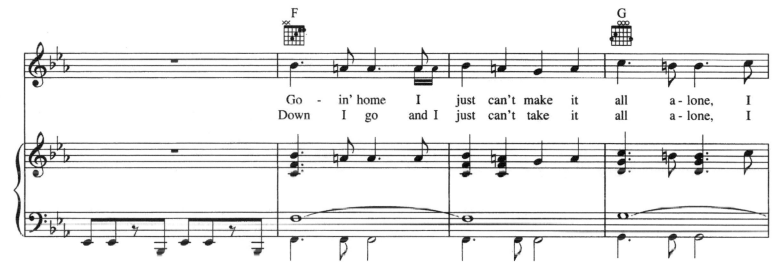

Go - in' home   I   just can't make   it   all   a - lone,   I
Down   I go   and I   just can't take   it   all   a - lone,   I

real - ly   should   be   hold - ing   you,   hold - ing   you,
real - ly   should   be   hold - ing   you,   hold - ing   you,

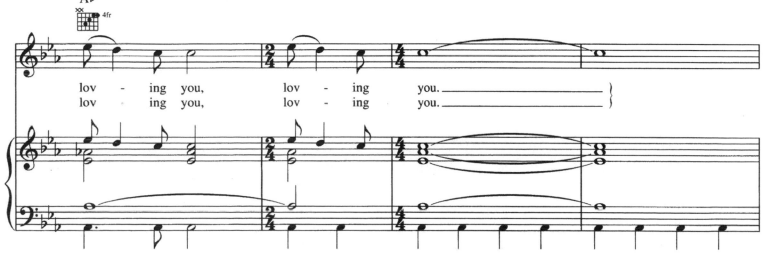

lov - ing   you,   lov - ing   you.
lov - ing   you,   lov - ing   you.

Trag - e - dy, _ when the feel - ing's gone and you can't go on, it's

trag - e - dy; _ when the morn - ing cries and you don't know why, it's

hard to bear _ with no one to love you you're go - in' no - where.

Trag - e - dy, _ when you lose con - trol and you got no soul, it's

178

trag - e - dy; ____ when the morn - ing cries and you don't know why, it's

hard to bear ____ with no one to love you you're go - in' no - where.

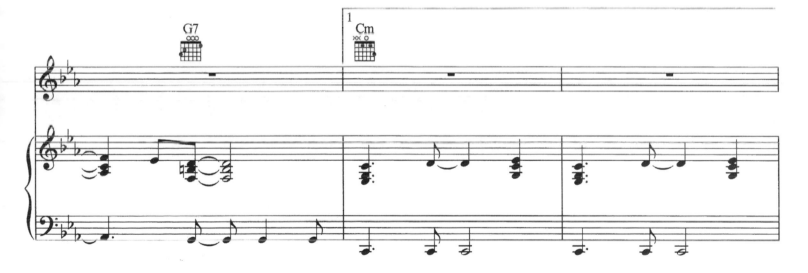

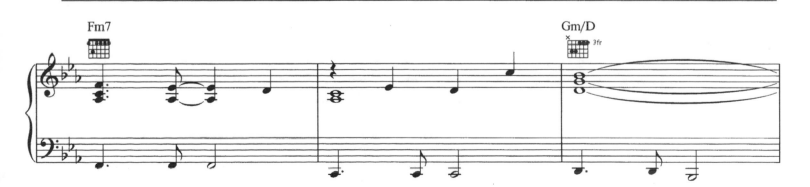

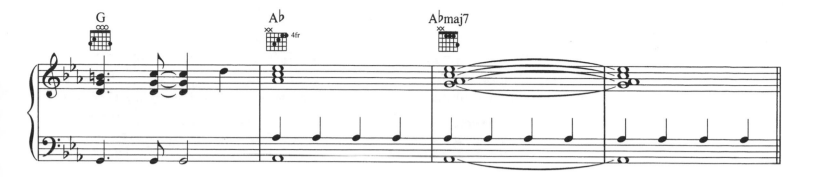

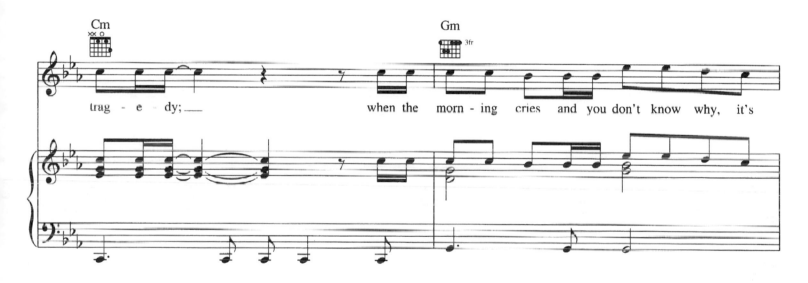

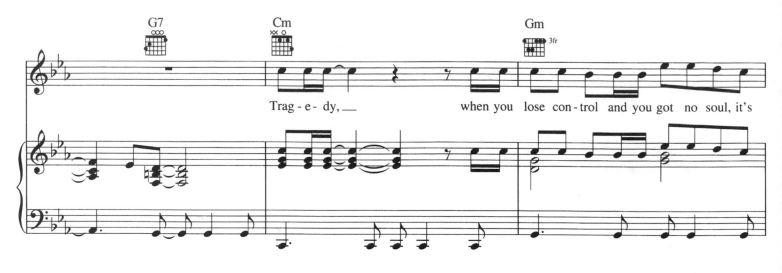

Trag-e-dy, ___ when you lose con-trol and you got no soul, it's

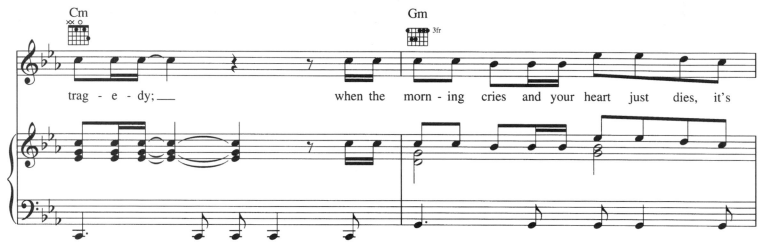

trag-e-dy; ___ when the morn-ing cries and your heart just dies, it's

hard to bear ___ with no one to love you you're

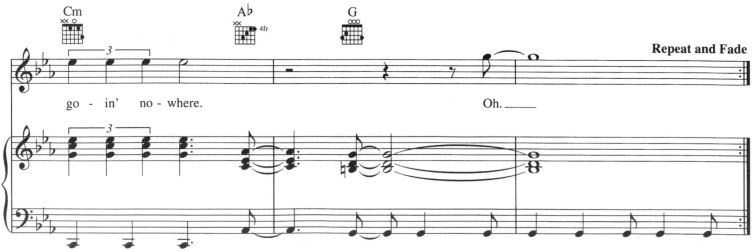

Repeat and Fade

go-in' no-where. Oh. ___

TAKE A CHANCE ON ME

Words & Music by Benny Andersson & Bjorn Ulvaeus

Capo 4th fret

Moderate steady four

If you change your mind___ I'm the first in line,___ ho-ney I'm still free,

___ take a chance on me,___ if you need me let___ me know, gon-na be a-round___

___ if you got no place___ to go when you're fee-ling down.

If you're all a - lone___ when the pre - tty birds___ have flown, ho - ney I'm still free,___

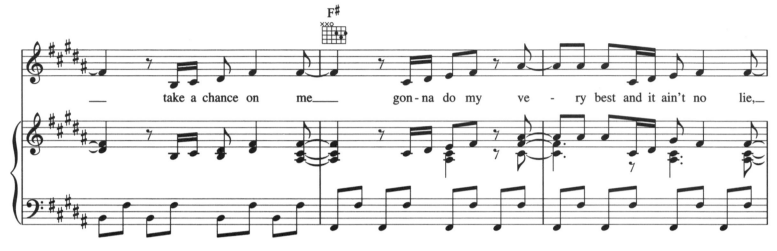

F#

take a chance on me___ gon - na do my ve - ry best and it ain't no lie,___

B

if you put me to___ the test, if you let me try,___ take a

C#m   F#   C#m

chance on me___ take a chance on me.___

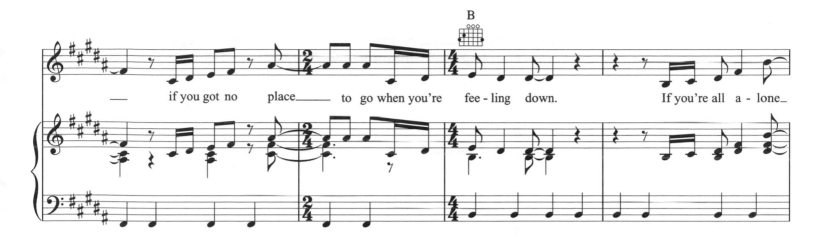

if you got no place___ to go when you're fee - ling down. If you're all a - lone__

___ when the pre - tty birds___ have flown, ho - ney I'm still free,___ take a chance on me__

___ gon - na do my ve - ry best baby, can't you see___ if you put me to__

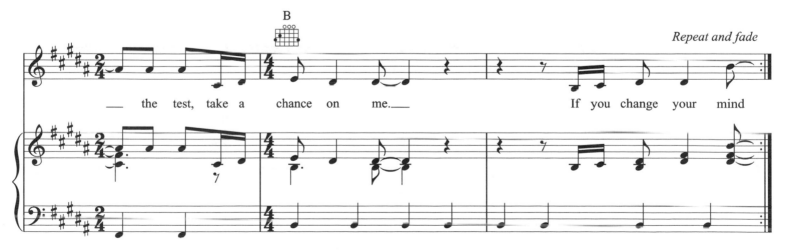

Repeat and fade

___ the test, take a chance on me.___ If you change your mind

WANNABE

Words & Music by Matt Rowe, Richard Stannard, Melanie Brown,
Victoria Adams, Geri Halliwell, Emma Bunton & Melanie Chisholm

I wan-na, I wan-na, I wan-na, I wan-na real-ly real-ly real-ly wan-na zig-a-zig ha.

1. If you want my fu-ture, for-get my past. If you wan-na get with me,
(Verse 2 see block lyric)

bet-ter make it fast.— Now don't go wast-ing my pre-cious time,

get your act to-ge - ther, we could be just— fine.— I'll

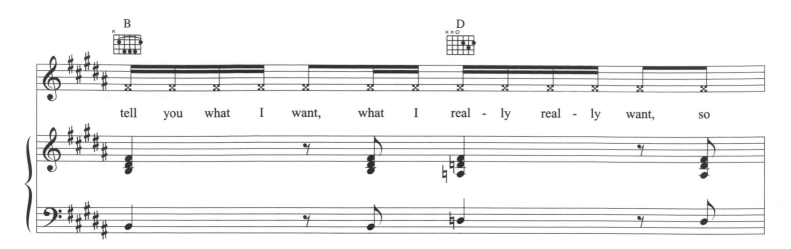

tell you what I want, what I real-ly real-ly want, so

tell me what you want, what you real-ly real-ly want. I wan-na,

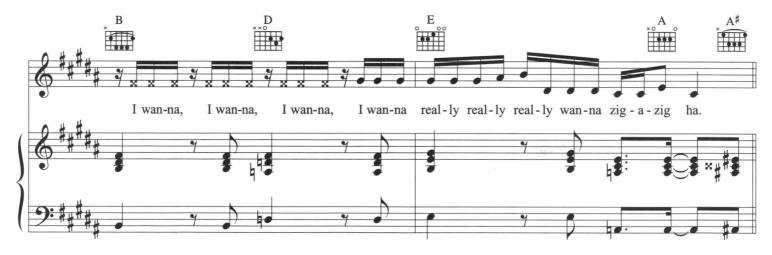

I wan-na, I wan-na, I wan-na, I wan-na real-ly real-ly real-ly wan-na zig-a-zig ha.

If you wan-na be my lov-er, you got-ta get with my friends.

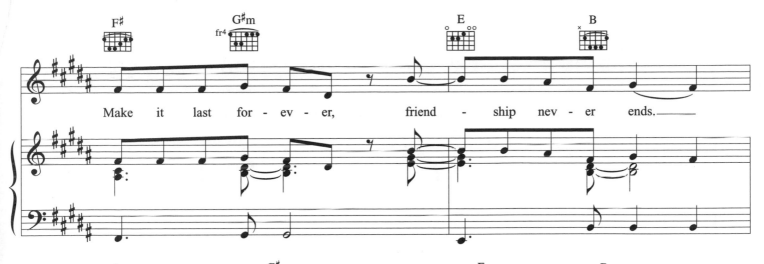

Make it last for - ev - er, friend - ship nev - er ends.____

If you wan - na be my lov - er, you have got to give,

1, 3.   *To Coda* ⊕

tak - ing is too ea - sy, but that's____ the way it is.____

2.

(2° vocal ad lib.)

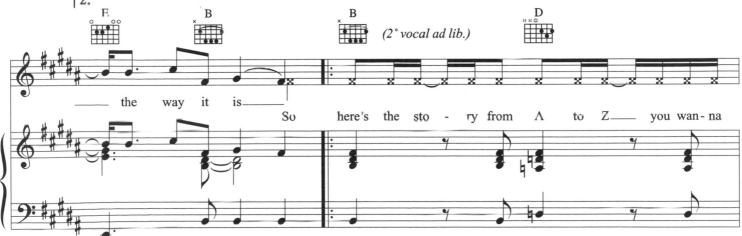

____ the way it is____ So here's the sto - ry from A to Z____ you wan - na

get with me,— you got-ta lis-ten care-ful-ly. You got M. in the place who likes— it in your face, you got

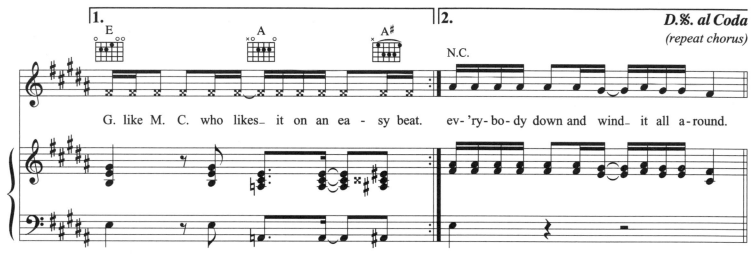

1.
G. like M. C. who likes— it on an ea - sy beat.

2.

D.%. al Coda
(repeat chorus)

ev-'ry-bo-dy down and wind— it all a-round.

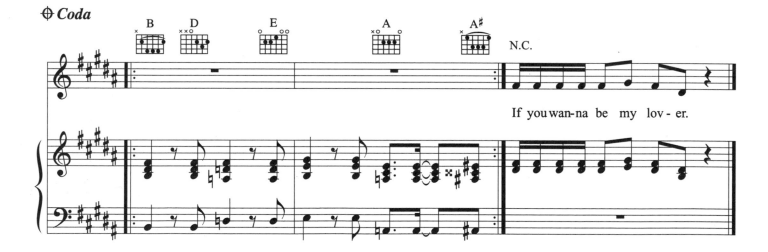

⊕ *Coda*

If you wan-na be my lov - er.

Verse 2:
What do you think about that now you know how I feel
Say you can handle my love, are you for real?
I won't be hasty, I'll give you a try
If you really bug me then I'll say goodbye.

123456789